Make Your Choices Better Than Chance: Here's How to Get it Right
(Second Edition)

For information about this title or to order other books and/or electronic media, contact the publisher.

ISBN: 978-0-578-70316-9
Printed in the United States of America

Book Design
David J. Kinsey, Alexander & Sydney, Redlands, California

Cover design
Mark Docker and Russ Potter

Center for Research on K-12 Adventist Education
4500 Riverwalk Parkway
Riverside, California 92505

DEDICATION

Posthumously to John (Jack) R. Thornbury, M.D., a friend and mentor who introduced me to the field of medical decision-making. He also demonstrated that the HOPE (helping-others -oriented people) worldview could be used effectively in the workplace.

Posthumously, to Graham Maxwell, Ph.D., who through his works clearly articulated and advocated the HOPE worldview.

ACKNOWLEDGMENTS

I am indebted to my wife, Elissa Kido, for her encouragement, criticisms and editing throughout the development of this book. Robert Cruise and Udo Oyoyo both critiqued the Decision Model during its early development. In addition, Robert Cruise introduced me to the traits associated with various personality types.

Melissa Brotton, Heather Reifsnyder, and Kenneth McFarland helped edit the book. Extensive editing was done by Clifford Goldstein, Sandra Blackmer and Aimee Leukert.

The cover was designed by Mark Docker and Russ Potter. Cindy Low Davi and Russ Potter helped with the title. The book was designed by David J. Kinsey of Alexander and Sydney.

I am also grateful to my friends who read the manuscript and made suggestions that improved the text and its readability. These include Sheri Harder, Douglas Havens, Paul Jacobson, Walter Johnson, David Larsen, Deborah Leonard, Martie Parsley and Barry Taylor.

contents

Chapter 2

Chapter 3

Chapter 4

Chapter 5

Chapter 6

preface

As a neuroscientist, I have spent many years exploring firsthand the wonders of the human mind. Our brains are truly unbelievable in their anatomical and physiological makeup, their resiliency, and their ability to analyze, compare, and filter the immense amount of information that pours into them daily from our five senses. And yet somehow, despite these tremendous capabilities, we still manage to make poor decisions! In fact, after studying this subject for decades, I believe that for most of us our chances of making good decisions are literally 50:50 at best!

How is it that we have been gifted with the potential to think critically and make good choices for ourselves, but still find ourselves failing time and time again?

Consider these notorious bad decisions:

- In 1962 Decca Records rejected the audition of a new pop group called The Beatles.
- In 1977, 20th Century Fox signed over the product rights of all *Star Wars* films to George Lucas for $20,000. Since then, merchandise sales from *Star Wars* has topped three billion dollars and continues to grow.
- Because Pete Rose bet on baseball games, in 1989 he was banned from having any contact with Major League Baseball. He was also denied entry into the Baseball Hall of Fame even though he holds the all-time hit record and was an all-star 17 times.

There is frequently *a significant difference* between the good choices we think we're making and the actual outcomes of those choices. The crux of this book is not just to help us understand why we make bad decisions, but more important, how we can make better ones.

We don't have to live with bad decisions if we can understand the relationship between worldviews and decision-making (choices). Chapter 1 lays the groundwork for this book by showing how worldviews impact our choice. Chapter 2 discusses the predictable outcomes that stem from those decisions. Chapter 3 describes which worldview will result in better decisions, while Chapter 4 highlights why one worldview is more advantageous than the others. Chapter 5 describes a variety of biases/thinking anomalies that are related to the various worldviews and that limit good decision-making. Finally, Chapter 6 explains how to change to a HOPE (helping-others-oriented people) worldview, one that can ensure good decision-making.

The 2nd edition differs from the 1st edition in the following two major ways:

(1) The me-first worldview has been divided into two worldviews: feelings-first and me-first worldviews. In figures 8, 9, and 10 feeling-first has been placed opposite rules-first, a position previously held by me-first. In turn, in figure 10 me-first has been relocated opposite others-first.

(2) The title **zone of uncertainty** previously described in chapter 1 has been changed to **contemplative zone** to be consistent with the process of change described in chapter 6.

chapter 1

How Worldviews Affect Decision-Making

The Lady or the Tiger?

In 1882, *Century* magazine published Frank Stockton's short story "The Lady or the Tiger." It told of an ancient king who had devised a uniquely barbaric method of justice. When a major offense had been committed, the accused was brought to an arena before an enormous crowd of onlookers, similar to the notorious Roman Coliseum. Two large, ominous doors stood at one end of the arena. The criminal was thrown into the arena with a single choice to make.

"He could open either door he pleased; he was subject to no guidance or influence but that of the aforementioned impartial and incorruptible chance. If he opened the one, there came out of it a hungry tiger, the fiercest and most cruel that could be procured, which immediately sprang upon him and tore him to pieces as a punishment for his guilt."[1]

The other door, however, held a different fate: "But, if the accused person opened the other door, there came forth from it a lady, the most suitable to his years and station that his majesty could select among his fair subjects, and to this lady he was immediately married, as a reward of his innocence. It mattered not that he might already possess a wife and family, or that his affections might be engaged upon an object of his own selection; the king allowed no such subordinate arrangements to interfere with his great scheme of retribution and reward."

Thus, depending on the accused's choice, he would get either the lady or the tiger.

The king had a beautiful daughter who caught the eye of a man far below her royal status. They fell in love, stealing away to meet with each other whenever they could. As clandestine as they were, they could not escape the king's surveillance. When the king learned of the secret courtship, he had the man arrested and sentenced to face the doors of the arena.

"The youth was immediately cast into prison, and a day was appointed for his trial in the king's arena. This, of course, was an especially important occasion, and his majesty, as well as all the people, were greatly interested in the trial. Never before had such a case occurred; never before had a subject dared to love the daughter of the king. In after years such things became commonplace enough, but then they were in no slight degree novel and startling."

In the audience that day was the king's daughter. The princess had a secret of her own; using the wiles that only princesses seem to possess, she had managed to uncover the secret of the doors. She knew with absolute certainty behind which door stood the lady and which the tiger.

But the princess had a dilemma. She knew that the lady behind the door was one of the most beautiful in the land, with locks of gold and eyes that captivated all whom she met. Moreover, the princess had already caught this woman exchanging playful glances with her beloved. Oh, how she'd burned at the sight of that! And now this enchantress was behind the arena door! "With all the intensity of the savage blood transmitted to her through long lines of wholly barbaric ancestors," Stockton wrote, "she hated the woman who blushed and trembled behind that silent door."

The time came. Her lover approached the doors, head bowed, a picture of resignation. He ventured one last look at his beloved princess and was startled at the look of knowing in her eyes. He could tell that she knew! She knew which door held life and which held death. She knew. With quiet confidence, the princess made a tiny gesture, "raised her hand, and made a slight, quick movement toward the right." The young man unhesitatingly grasped at this lifeline and chose the door on the right.

What fate did the princess choose for her lover? Would she rather see her lover clawed to death by the tiger or in the arms of another woman, one whom she hated with a passion?

"The Lady or the Tiger" by Asa Nemoto

Stockton ends the story like this:

"Her decision had not been indicated in an instant, but it had been made after days and nights of anguished deliberation. She had known she would be asked, she had decided what she would answer, and, so now, without the slightest hesitation, she had moved her hand to the right.

"The question of her decision is one not to be lightly considered, and it is not for me to presume to set myself up as the one person able to answer it. And so I leave it with all of you: Which came out of the opened door—the lady, or the tiger?"

Making Choices

There are a number of theories about Stockton's ending; some readers are wholly unsatisfied with the lack of definitive closure, while others are convinced that the princess fed her lover to the tiger, still others feel she chose life for her lover, even if it placed him in the arms of a woman she hated. Whatever one might think of Stockton's ending, he does make a powerful point regarding the importance of the choices that we make.

The dilemma presented in "The Lady or the Tiger" sets the stage for this book: the choices we make and how we make them. We all live in our own arena every day, faced with our own sets of doors. We have to make decisions every day and we search our surroundings, looking for more information, looking for telltale signs that will help us choose the right door. Without adequate knowledge, however, our choices are arbitrary, left only to chance.

What principles, what criteria and what worldview did she use to determine whether her lover would end up in the jaws of a hungry tiger or in the embrace of her rival? What did she choose? What should she have chosen?

To most of us, it seems like the rational choice would be life for her lover. True love, we muse, makes us want to see our beloved alive, fulfilled, content—not mauled by a wild beast. However, while we are all capable of making rational decisions, most of us are not like Mr. Spock, the Vulcan of *Star Trek* fame, who made only rational, fact-based decisions.

So how do we choose? What do we rely on when making decisions?

Choices, Choices, Choices

Life is full of choices. Every day we make choices: big choices, little choices, short-term and long-term choices. Between the time we wake in the morning and decide whether or not to hit snooze one more time to when we finally collapse into bed, promising ourselves that we'll wake up earlier the next day in order to get more done—we have to make decision after decision after decision. A recent study out of Columbia University reported that adults make more than 70 significant decisions each day![2]

So how do we make the choices we do? What criteria do we use to make choices—choices that, when pieced together, determine who we are and the kinds of lives we live?

The idea behind this book is simple: despite the great and still-ongoing debate about free will and despite the reality of variables and circumstances that we cannot control, we human beings every day are confronted with the reality of choice. Unfortunately, this ability to choose comes with a hefty price tag; hence, Jean Paul Sartre's famous quote: "Man is condemned to be free." Yes, we are able to choose but with those choices come the determination of our destiny.

In the pages that follow, we are going to explore a powerful idea about how to make the best possible choices. In addition, we will try to understand why some decisions we've made did not turn out as we expected in order to help us make better choices in the future.

The Most Important Choice

When I ask the question, "What is the most important decision you will make in your lifetime?" the answer varies and is highly dependent on age. Teenagers fret about choosing the right college, graduates wring their hands over the right career, and retirees contemplate how they will live out their last decades.

But let's spend some time unpacking just one of life's biggest decisions—marriage. Couples in a dating relationship often seek advice about their significant other and the future they will have together. They might ask their friends: "What do you think of us?" "Is he/she the right one?" Or they might go to their parents or grandparents for counsel and ask, "How do I know?" They might study relationship books, read pop culture magazines or even sift through advice columns for information relevant to their current situation.

And yet for all their efforts to make the best decision about their future life partner, divorce statistics show that the odds of first marriages working out are only 50:50! Why is it that despite their best intentions and efforts almost 50 percent of first-time marriages result in divorce?

If the outcome of this big decision is no better than our chances at winning a coin toss, then we are like those prisoners standing before the two closed doors in the king's arena. How do you feel about making the next important decision of your life, maybe even the most important one—knowing you have a 50 percent chance of being wrong?

Surely, we can—and must—find a better way to make our decisions.

Father and Two Sons

There is another story, one going back millennia to the ancient Near East, that can help us better understand the process behind making good decisions.[3]

The story begins on a prosperous farm—a wealthy family, lots of property, lots of servants and hired help. The owner of the farm, who has two sons, is well respected in the community: known for his goodness and generosity, not just with his own workers but with strangers, as well.

The younger son has a vivacious and winsome personality; he's handsome, optimistic and certain that life will give him what he pleases. The father observes that this son thinks quite highly of himself, is proud of his appearance and struts around the farm like some of his roosters. He catches him stealing glances at his own reflection to make certain everything is in place. The younger son stops passing caravans to peruse the latest clothing styles. The attention he pays to grooming himself, the father thinks ruefully, could be far better spent learning how to run the farm. However, the younger son puts very little effort into his work and does just enough to get by. He has no drive, no enthusiasm, and no desire to build-up the farm.

The older brother, in contrast, is quiet and reserved. But while he may not be outgoing or witty, he doesn't hold back when it comes to criticism or judgment of others. The older brother also thinks highly of himself, not about his features and dress, but about the right way he does things. He works hard and expects those around him to work equally hard. Goodwill should be earned, he reasons. He chides his father for being overly generous with his servants, farmhands, and especially his brother.

As the younger son grew, he became more and more restless. Life on the farm was constricting; he wanted to see more of the world, to live a more exciting life. By the time he reaches young adulthood, he had made up his mind. He was going to Damascus, a city miles away where he would pursue more sophisticated friends and live a life of glitz and glamour.

One day, after being asked to feed the pigs for the umpteenth time, the younger son exploded and rashly demanded his share of the inheritance. "I want what's coming to me now!" he insisted. "I want to pursue my destiny while I'm still young. I want out of here!"

Though saddened by his son's outburst, the father knew that there was no convincing him otherwise, no changing the boy's mind. So, he reluctantly conceded and watched his son dance down the road, gold in hand, without a backward glance.

In contrast to the father, the older brother was glad to be rid of the "jerk" (although he never said it quite like that to his father).

As time passed, the older brother occasionally noticed his father looking wistfully down the road where his brother had gone, but rather than comforting him, he silently scoffed at him. In fact, the older brother would occasionally ask his father if he had heard from his brother but only to take the opportunity to tell his father that they were better off without him.

A Turn of Events

The father would have been happy to hear that his younger son was doing well in Damascus. Sadly, however, that wasn't the case. The younger son had answered the siren call of the glamorous life and was indeed living large in the big city. His nights were spent hopping from party to party—alcohol at one, drugs at another. He slept it off during the day, rousing himself as evening fell only to repeat it all over again.

Living the good life took money, lots of it, and without any income, the young man's inheritance began to shrink. He recognized this reality all too late when one night, he was kicked out of a bar for not having enough cash to cover his charges.

He felt bewildered, lost. How had this happened? His share of the inheritance had been so large! Where had it all gone? The young man remained hopeful. "All I need is a job," he reassured himself. "Just an easy 9-to-5 clock-in, clock-out and I'll be back on track." But the country was in a recession and jobs were scarce. No one, it seemed, wanted to hire a young inexperienced man with only farming experience.

The young man eventually ran out of cash. He sold his clothes, his jewels, then his furniture and, finally, his house.

He soon realized that his newfound friends were just as quick to abandon him as they had been to enjoy his money. In desperation, he knocked on one door after another. Surely, they'd remember the life of the party! But time and time again, he was turned away or even worse, ignored.

With no leads in the city, the young man eventually left Damascus, looking for a job, any job, even a farm job for a little food.

Finally, after innumerable rejections, a farmer showed him to the back of his barn and gruffly said, "I could use someone back here with the pigs." He rattled off instructions: collect scraps from the compost bin, feed the pigs twice a day, and muck out the stalls each evening. Swallowing hard, the young man nodded and reached for the shovel hoping to earn enough to buy food.

Living in filth, surrounded by grunting, greedy pigs, the younger son had to confront his current reality. He also reflected on his decisions: the depth of his friendships in Damascus, his unrealistic dreams of the good life, the family he had left behind. As he shoveled in new straw and cleaned out the pigs' troughs, he couldn't help but recognize the irony of his situation: the life he'd run from, the life that he'd considered boring and sheltered and limited. Oh, what he would give to get it back!

As the weeks and then months passed, the young man began to realize that he was starving, in spite of supplementing his diet with bits of food intended for the pigs. He finally decided to swallow his pride and try to get a job back home before it was too late. He would beg his father for a job, any job, and promise to be a hard-working employee. Given his track record, he realized his father might not believe him or even consider his plea, but if he were to survive he had to try.

The Homecoming

And so he trudged back home. The despondent young man's appearance was a far cry from how he looked when he left eons ago. Neighboring farmers raised their eyebrows at this unkempt, gaunt, stranger as he passed by. They also held their noses since he smelled! He smelled of pigs!

At just that very moment, his father was out mending the fence in the front of his house. It had become a habit for him to glance down the road every now and again, searching hopefully for any sign of his son. A few years had passed and yet he still looked, to no avail. Until now!

The sun hung low as he scanned the horizon, and at first he wondered if it was just the odd reflection catching on a fence post. What was this? Could it be? The gaunt unkempt stranger with slumped shoulders and uncertain gait surely wasn't his son . . . was it? The father stood up straight and squinted. His heart began to race as the traveler drew nearer. Without waiting another moment he began walking and then running down the road. As he approached, the younger son put out his arms, as if to ward off any recriminations.

"Wait, Father, let me explain" he began, stumbling over the words he'd rehearsed again and again on his journey home.

But before he could get his proposal out, his father engulfed him in an embrace. "My son, my son!" he gasped, overcome with emotion. "You've come home!"

He threw his robe over his son's shoulders, covering up the torn rags he was wearing, and ran his trembling fingers through the boy's hair, smoothing the tangles. He grasped the younger son's face in both hands, staring in awe and wonder at the miracle standing before him. Then he snapped into action, shouting instructions to his servants as he rushed the boy into the main house.

"Prepare a feast! We're having a party! My son has come home!" he shouted.

Just about this time, the older brother was returning home from a day out in the fields. Even from a distance, he noticed the increased activity at the house. Servants scurried about, and their chatter held a tone of excitement. A farmhand trotted by, carrying a squirming young calf. The older brother caught him by the arm and demanded, "What's all this? Where are you going with that? My father had that calf marked for a special occasion!" The servant adjusted his grasp on the calf and replied impatiently, "This is a special occasion—we're having a party! Haven't you heard? Your brother is home!"

Shocked, the older brother released the servant and took a step back. Home? His brother? What nerve! What was his father thinking? His younger brother had probably squandered away his inheritance and come back looking for more. "But he isn't going to get any more, not if I can help it," the older brother fumed. He was going to put a stop to this! The angry older brother stomped into the house.

"Father! Father! What's this all about?"

The father met his older son in the doorway and waited patiently through his barrage of indignant protests. "I have been slaving away for you all this time. I did not demand a penny from you. I am the responsible, trustworthy, obedient one. How come you haven't thrown a party for me?"

The father tried to reason with him, "Son—you have always been here and you know that everything I possess is yours." But the older son wouldn't listen and elected not to attend the party.

I have long pondered this story, wrestling with the implications of what it means to me.

Decisions, Decisions

I believe this story presents us with an excellent model of three different approaches to decision-making.

The younger son learned that the lifestyle he'd so eagerly sought was just a utopian fantasy. The dreams he had for his future were radically different from the reality he actually experienced. It appears as if he came home a changed man—humbler, more introspective, more grateful.

The older son did not, however, seem to have learned any lessons during his brother's absence. On the contrary, he appeared to have become even more judgmental and arrogant. Rather than feeling any sympathy or gratitude that his younger brother had returned, he was instead more concerned with the impact his brother's return might have on his own inheritance.

And, finally, there's the father—a picture of grace and unconditional love. He didn't chastise the younger son on his return, didn't belittle him with "I told you so." Instead, he embraced, he welcomed, and he loved. Neither did he condemn his older son for his arrogance and callousness.

The three characters in this study made very different decisions, each resulting in such different outcomes. Let's analyze this story to learn what we can about decision-making.

The Decision-Making Process

Let's start by unpacking the process of decision-making.

Decision-making can often be a quick, reflexive reaction depending on our memory of a similar situation. Sometimes, however, it can be deliberate, as outlined in Figure 1.

Our decisions are made, of course in our heads, our brains and our minds. The genesis of deliberate decision-making occurs when either our consciousness faces a problem or our subconscious becomes aware of a need.

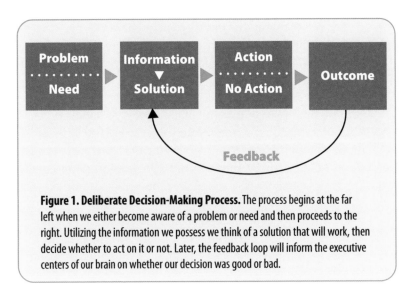

Figure 1. Deliberate Decision-Making Process. The process begins at the far left when we either become aware of a problem or need and then proceeds to the right. Utilizing the information we possess we think of a solution that will work, then decide whether to act on it or not. Later, the feedback loop will inform the executive centers of our brain on whether our decision was good or bad.

In seeking a solution to a problem/need, our mind will come up with several options, all of which it thinks are reasonable and will have a good outcome that will make us feel good.[4, 5] Our mind will then simulate the various options; meaning, it will think through the possible outcomes resulting from each option and then select the one that it thinks has the best possibility of succeeding and at the same time optimizing our well-being. The decision-making part of our brain then tells the rest of the body to act; that is, it says: This is the choice that I've made. It's going to have a good outcome, so let's get going.

In contrast, if our mind thinks that solution will fail, it will reject it.

Consider this simple scenario: Your boss emails you in the morning with a request for a meeting with you that afternoon. He seldom springs last minute appointments on you, so you assume it must be important.

You have several choices here. You could:

a) ignore the request and delete the email;
b) acknowledge the request, but make up an excuse for not being able to attend;
c) reply that you look forward to meeting with him/her, but then skip the meeting and go home;
d) ask a colleague what to do;
e) respond affirmatively and meet with him;
     …and the list goes on!

There are myriad ways that you could choose to handle this situation and, miraculously, your brain sorts through all of them in seconds. Without knowing you or your context, my guess would be that you would reject options a, b, or c. Chances are you want to keep your job, and because you realize those choices would not help with that outcome, your brain will throw them out.

Far too often, however, the choice that looks and feels good ends up being so wrong. I can think of many, many times in my life when I convinced myself that I was making the right decision and yet it all still went south.

So what can we do to help make future choices that will, indeed, turn out well?

That's where our feedback loop comes in. After each decision a part of our brain evaluates the result of our action and determines whether the outcome was good or bad, much like a good student might reflect on the results of his math test and work out the problems that he missed in anticipation that he might see them again on the final examination. Similarly, our brain stores the results from our previous choices for future use. When it spots a similar decision, it whips out the appropriate piece of information and applies it.

In short, we learn from both our successes and mistakes if our feedback loop is working properly. The younger son's feedback loop, although functioning suboptimally, let him know that he was starving to death. On the other hand, the older son's feedback loop appeared to be dysfunctional.

Worldviews

If we want to avoid bad decisions, we need to add one more very important piece to the flow diagram on decision-making in Figure 1 and that would be *worldview* (Figure 2).

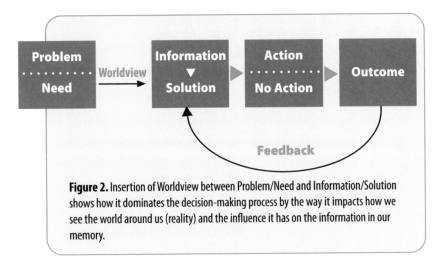

Figure 2. Insertion of Worldview between Problem/Need and Information/Solution shows how it dominates the decision-making process by the way it impacts how we see the world around us (reality) and the influence it has on the information in our memory.

The story of the father and two sons speaks directly to this observation. They each had a different worldview, and that is what determined their choices and the subsequent results.

What is a worldview? It's exactly that—it's how we view the world. It's the lens through which we interpret the reality that we experience.

When I was a child I had lots of toys at my disposal: bouncing balls, a rocking horse, gadgets that spun or made noise or flashed blinking lights. But one of the things I was most intrigued by did not reside in my toy chest but was often perched on my grandmother's nose: her glasses. Whenever I found them on a table or bureau, I would put them on. The ear loops were too big and the frame too large for my face, but oh, how I loved playing with them. I was intrigued at how the world *changed* when I looked out through those glasses. Lines that were clear were now blurry and at other times the images seemed nauseatingly distorted. I would flip them up and down, up and down, totally fascinated at the sudden change in perspective that each movement produced.

Glasses do alter how we view the world, don't they? What if, instead of a pair of glasses that changed the physical clarity of our vision, we each owned a pair of glasses that changed how we viewed reality? What if our glasses made beautiful people ugly? What if they turned a generous act into a selfish one?

In some ways, that's what a worldview does. We look through our worldview "glasses" and we see the reality they present. Our worldview provides us a way to understand life and, as a result, it is the tool we use to make decisions.

I propose that a worldview, like a pair of glasses, is central to the decision-making process that we are seeking to understand in this book.[6,7,8]

Another way to understand worldviews is to compare it to a computer's operating system. You put data in and what comes out depends, really, on its operating system. The Microsoft operating system gives us one outcome, while the Macintosh system gives us a different outcome.

Worldviews do that to us, as well.

Most of us develop our worldview unconsciously as we grow. We don't wake up one day and say, *"Self, I think it's time we adopted a post-modern feminist worldview."* Rather, our minds are constantly being shaped by ideas and experiences from our interactions with our parents, teachers, friends, faith traditions, employers, books, and—possibly most important today—the media.[9] Research shows that most children form the rudiments of their worldview by the age of 13.[10]

How many worldviews are there? Some say there are as many worldviews as there are religions, but I believe even that estimate is too narrow, given that many other factors besides faith influence our thinking.

Scientists and social theorists have created a vast array of worldviews.

Philosophers and theologians have created a variety of worldviews.

Economists, biologists, historians, ethicists—all have also created their own worldviews.

Worldviews also affect nations: observe the variety of governments we have throughout the world. As social groups evolve, they also develop new worldviews. In the 1960s, for example, Western societies moved to the era of post-modernity and began placing a higher value on relativism and multi-culturism. In turn, this has resulted in a proliferation and fragmentation of viewpoints, many times resulting in special-interest groups that run the danger of having tunnel vision.

For example, those individuals and groups interested in social justice began the anti-discrimination movement that in turn spawned the feminist and gay-rights groups. The environmentalists began with global warming and the concern for excess carbon dioxide production that then fragmented into save the whales and on the West Coast to save the redwoods, the coast-line, and wetlands.

The equally fascinating and terrifying part about worldviews is that, by and large, there's some truth to all of them. The problem, however, is that some truth becomes, for their proponents, the whole truth. In the process of bridging the gap between some truth and total truth, most worldviews create a false reality, one that leads people to make wrong choices. We will examine that issue more closely in later chapters.

The foundation of this book rests on my assertion that worldviews, despite their vast proliferation, can be sorted into four major groups. There are certainly many differences within each group, but these four groups encapsulate the major themes that are common to that worldview.

Following is a brief introduction to those four worldviews:

ROPE Group

Rules-oriented people (ROPE) adopt a set of values that they think is absolute truth and seek information that confirms their beliefs. People with a ROPE worldview support traditional social values and norms and have a high respect for authority. Familiar routines, known expectations, make them feel comfortable which can be the root of bad decisions.

Elementary school teachers prize ROPE students. Their report cards might include statements like, "Bob is a joy to teach. He follows all the classroom rules and is a good listener." If a term paper is supposed to be 15 pages long, the ROPE student's paper will be 15 pages not a sentence more, not a sentence less.

ROPE individuals have a highly developed sense of fairness because they know the rules. If you're playing a game with them, you can rely on them knowing and following the rules.

The weakness in the ROPE worldview, however, is that in order to escape uncertainty they can distort or misinterpret reality, leading them to make bad decisions. For example, in the story of the father and his two sons, the older brother sacrificed the bond he might have developed with his younger brother for the exacting price of the rules he had adopted.

FOPE Group

The "feelings-first" oriented people (FOPE) believe that their personal values gives them license to pursue pleasure even if it injures others. These people often act impulsively and irresponsibly in their attempt to feel "alive." They believe they know what is right for their lives, regardless of conventional wisdom or the viewpoints of others and insist on forging their own paths, like the younger son. "Tradition is for the birds," they cry. In former times they were known as Hedonists. In more recent times they were known as Hippies or the "flower children" of the 1960s. Some millennials fall into this group.

FOPE thinkers are swayed by their desires and emotions. They're the first to catapult off a waterfall, first to slam down their glass in a drinking bet, first to drop money into a financial investment.

With this worldview, the "rational" choice is the one that produces the most immediate pleasure. However, they might be admonished to "look before they leap."

MOPE Group

The me-first oriented group (MOPE) is composed of people who have adopted the theory of the "survival of the fittest" and selectively adopted elements of the ROPE and MOPE worldview that they think will help them get ahead. They are less rules oriented than the ROPE group and are more disciplined than the FOPE group. Regardless, their underlying motivations are money and power because of the status it gives them.

Consider those politicians who change their position depending upon the results from the latest poll. They see themselves as clever and adaptable, but others as they get to know them think they are unprincipled and untrustworthy.

Individuals with the MOPE worldview may be highly social and thrive in the spotlight where their uniqueness can be confirmed by others. Some individuals in this group may become successful entrepreneurs because of their ability to sell their ideas to others. Others in this group can command a room with their strong presence; others draw people through their charming personalities.

Because of these characteristics, some MOPEs become wealthy. However, this may not always be good or desirable. An article in the *Wall Street Journal* titled "Don't Envy the Super-rich, They Are Miserable" reported that one study showed "the ultra-rich as lost souls burdened by the fears, worries, and family distortions of too much money."[11] It quoted another study that said "the respondents turn out to be a generally dissatisfied lot, whose money has contributed to deep anxieties involving love, work, and family. Indeed, they are frequently dissatisfied even with their sizable fortunes. Most of them do not consider themselves financially secure; for that, they say, they would require on average one-quarter more wealth than they currently possess." Some of these people net at least 25 million dollars annually, and yet they still don't feel they have enough![11] Happiness is elusive when pursued from a MOPE approach.

HOPE Group

Helping-others-oriented people (HOPE) value their relationships with others. In their decisions, they intentionally look for options that yield better, stronger relationships. HOPE thinkers base their actions on how they can positively affect others as opposed to just themselves.

HOPE individuals excel at looking at the big picture. Rather than getting bogged down by trivial details or short-term consequences, they have the ability to zero in on the heart of the matter, the most important issue, caring for others. They care about others' feelings, about the effects of their own actions, about the well-being of those around them. In this process they are careful to not infringe upon the freedom of others.

Just like the ROPE and MOPE followers, HOPE individuals also weigh the pros and cons of their choices. They, too, have to determine what the best possible outcome is for their decisions; the difference is that "best" for them means "best" for others as well.

Listen to these words of wisdom:

- "Live simply so others may simply live."
- "I can do things you cannot, you can do things I cannot; together we can do great things."
- "It is a kingly act to assist the fallen."
- "If you can't feed a hundred people, then feed just one."
- "I want you to be concerned about your next-door neighbor. Do you know your next-door neighbor?"
- "Spread love everywhere you go. Let no one ever come to you without leaving happier."

Good words to live by, right? But do you know what I find so astounding about the above quotes? *They were all made by a single person.* A person who truly exemplified the HOPE worldview: Mother Teresa.[12] A person who truly valued helping others.

Two groups that *think* they are HOPEs consist of people who have combined HOPE with either a FOPE or ROPE worldview. People in the FOPE /HOPE group can be altruistic and well-meaning at one moment but can just as quickly put their own self-interest above others especially during times of stress. Take the outspoken environmentalists, for instance, who march at global warming rallies and protest the use of fossil fuel. Yet, while spouting platitudes about "global warming" and "climate change," they drive gas-guzzling RUVs and live in air-conditioned houses whose thermostats aren't turned down.

The ROPE/HOPE subgroup is comprised of people who struggle between putting others first and putting rules first. They *think* they are altruistic and unselfish, but if they could see themselves as others see them they would be shocked. Before and during the Civil War, many southern slaveholders who had ROPE/HOPE worldviews justified their ownership and treatment of black slaves by categorizing them as sub-humans who needed their protection. Some Christian slaveholders with ROPE/HOPE worldviews selectively picked biblical stories to justify their position. They spoke confidently about God's mercy towards them but failed to see the inconsistency in how they treated their slaves.

The problem with people who combine their worldviews with the HOPE worldview is that they deceive themselves into thinking that they are the people they wish to be by creating their own reality. They don't realize that they are corrupting their feedback loop, leading them to make poor choices based on those "glasses" that they wear.

Contemplative Zone

One of the most famous novels of the twentieth century was George Orwell's *1984*, his dystopian vision of a future in which the prevailing image of humanity was a boot on a human face.[13] Orwell wrote the book in the 1940s, and although his predictions have not entirely come true, nevertheless, the book to this day is still read and deemed pertinent. *1984* is about Winston Smith who had been arrested and tortured by the oppressive political system that Orwell envisioned was coming. In one scene, O'Brien, the interrogator, holds up before Winston four fingers and demands that Winston tell him that he is holding up five fingers. He doesn't want Winston to just tell him there are five fingers. No, he wants Winston to actually see five fingers because that's what he is telling him are there.

"You are a slow learner, Winston," said O'Brien gently.

"How can I help it?" Winston blubbered. "How can I help seeing what is in front of my eyes? Two and two are four."

"Sometimes, Winston. Sometimes they are five. Sometimes they are three. Sometimes they are all of them at the same time. You must try harder."

What is this strange scene about? It's about the loss of the very concept of truth. It's the idea that truth isn't objective or real. O'Brien was having difficulty convincing Winston to question his worldview and accept the idea that truth is a mere human cultural concept. He wanted Winston to accept the idea that truth is about what you feel, what you think, what you believe it to be. O'Brien understood that if he could get Winston to question his view of reality and get him into the *contemplative zone* he could change his view of reality.

Some individuals with a FOPE, ROPE or MOPE worldview see flaws in their current worldview and begin to contemplate alternate strategies for making better decisions. O'Brien was trying to get Winston to question his reality and enter the contemplative zone where he might be able to change Winston's worldview.[14]

We may enter the contemplative zone following reading a book that questions our worldview, a discussion in which we heard good arguments against our current worldview or in a class we are taking. The important idea is that when we are in the contemplative zone we have the possibility of changing to a more realistic worldview without compromising reality as O'Brien was asking Winston to do.

Flatland

In 1884, British mathematician and teacher Edwin Abbott published a satirical novel called *Flatland*.[15] Though originally a spoof on the hierarchy of Victorian culture, the book has been seen, and rightly so, as a way to challenge a person's, or even a whole culture's, narrow view of reality. In short, it can be seen as a book about worldviews and how resistant people are to change.

In his work, Abbott describes three unusual lands: Lineland, Flatland and Spaceland. The main character in the story, A Square, lives in Flatland (a two-dimensional land) where one's two-dimensional shape depends on one's social status. The residents of

Flatland look down on the inhabitants of Lineland who are all thin and straight and can only travel in a straight line, either forwards or backward.

One day, A Square ventures out beyond his land's boundaries into Spaceland. He is astounded that the residents there can travel in any direction they choose. He is even more amazed by their three-dimensional shapes; he never imagined people could come in so many sizes and shapes. He races (as quickly as a square can) back to Flatland, where he delivers an enthusiastic report to his family and friends. He doesn't even have words to describe these marvelous figures and the opportunities that exist there; but oh, how he tries. His fellow citizens, however, scoff at his story and eventually throw him into their mental hospital, convinced that he has lost his mind.

While it was written over a hundred years ago, *Flatland* is a modern version of the story Plato told centuries ago in *The Republic*.[16] Plato, like Abbott, poses this question: *Why are some people willing to embrace new ideas, while others reject and even suppress them?*

I think the answer is worldview. As we see in the citizens of Flatland, there is a danger in holding onto one's opinions too tightly and focusing on ideas and data from one limited perspective. We've already seen that different worldviews result in different outcomes, so the root of a good choice may lie in which worldview we hold. The question is are we willing to enter the contemplative zone.

Summary

So where am I going with all of this? My point, the point of this book, is that the worldview you choose, the pair of glasses you choose to wear, affects every aspect of your life, including, or maybe especially the decisions you make. Whichever of the four categories you may fall into is largely indicative of your priorities, your values and your relationships with others.

Like the older brother, many people who hold a ROPE worldview feel they have a contract with society. If they work hard, it is society's duty to reward them with an appropriate level of comfort and security. Furthermore, if they keep the rules their priests or pastors say are important to God, they feel that God is obligated to provide and protect them during their lives on earth, while reserving a place for them in heaven. In other words, they expect the world to work in a certain way, to follow certain rules, no matter what. When life doesn't fall neatly into place, the ROPEs may become bitter as they become skeptical about their worldview.

In contrast, there are the FOPEs, who, like the younger brother, are impulsively driven by their desire for immediate gratification. The resulting poor outcomes may result in either a more desperate attempt to gratify themselves or perhaps to question their worldview.

Those with a HOPE worldview, like the father, get their rewards as they develop meaningful relationships with others. Famous mathematician Albert Einstein once stated, "Only a life lived for others is worth living." That may as well be HOPE's mantra. For them, every interaction promises to be a source of satisfaction and helping others is another opportunity to develop deep, significant connections with those around them. HOPE followers often find that as they age, life has even more meaning, more purpose. On the flip side, those who have adopted one of the other three worldviews begin to slowly realize that the happiness they experience is fleeting. The MOPE worldview is not a part of the story of the father and his two sons because the evolutionary theory or anything similar to it had not yet been developed

With so much at stake, we need to pursue this concept of worldviews further. We may not think our choices are as grave as the lover in the arena, faced with a lady or a tiger and yet, is it not so? Are not the decisions that we make every day, every week, every year resulting in equally profound consequences?

We all have been granted one life to live, an indeterminate number of years in which to leave our mark on this earth. How can we make that life meaningful? How can we make the best decisions possible?

By choosing the right pair of glasses!

chapter 2

How Decision-Making Affects Outcomes

You've probably heard the famous story of Isaac Newton sitting under an apple tree and an apple falling on his head. Voila! With a clunk on his noggin, Newton "discovered" gravity. There's a good chance that this story is actually true, but it definitely didn't end there, as the ramifications of that discovery were much more complicated. You see, even in the 1600s, everyone already knew about gravity. What made Newton's epiphany significant was that he connected gravity, the force that caused the apple to fall on his head, with the force that kept the earth in orbit around the sun. He later realized that this was also the same power that explained the motion of the planets in our solar system and the stars in our galaxy.

Newton demonstrated that much of nature works by natural laws that, in turn, can be reduced to mathematical formulas. It was a pivotal moment for science and truly changed the entire intellectual history of the world.

His explanation of nature led to what people called the "clockwork universe," the idea that the whole universe is built like a clock. You wind it up and it moves according to predetermined rules and laws. A Frenchman named Pierre-Simon Laplace expanded the idea by arguing that if everything followed natural laws and if it were possible to know the position of every particle in the universe, it would be possible to predict the future. You could know exactly what was going to happen, not just in the world of inanimate objects, such as the weather and the motion of the stars, but also in what choices people would make. In essence, if Laplace's theory were true, humans would have no free will but, rather, would live a predetermined destiny.

Let's go to the other end of the spectrum. In 1918, Max Planck won the Nobel Prize in physics for his foundational work in discovering quantum mechanics, a concept that resulted in a similar revolution. Planck managed to turn classical physics, the physics of Newton's clockwork universe, on its head.

At its most simplistic level, the gist of quantum physics is that reality is unpredictable. Certain things happen with no real reason for them to happen. It's not that we don't know the reason; there is no reason. At this level, everything happens purely by chance.

Two opposing viewpoints: one that states that there is a rule and reason behind everything and one that argues there is no rationale behind anything. Both of these paradigms are used as arguments against free will.

This book, however, is based on the assumption that regardless of the forces around us or even in us, we have the power of choice. We have the power to make decisions.

I believe we *do* have free will, especially where it counts—and that is in the crucial choices we make that determine the course of our lives. The quality of our lives, the quality of our relationships, the essence of our whole existence, depends upon our choices. So how do we stack the odds in our favor in terms of decision-making? This comes back around to the crux of this book: *What are the factors that determine the kind of choices we make?*

Before we more closely examine how to make better choices, let's first explore the types of mistakes that can occur in our decision-making process.

Two Types of Errors

Going back to the story in Chapter 1 about the father and his two sons, the brothers made two different errors: Type I and Type II. While this is fairly standard jargon in the world of scientific research, I think it makes for an interesting application here as well.

But first let's talk about these two types of errors. In any statistics course, students learn that making Type I errors means to mistake *something for nothing*. You believe there is a relationship between two different variables when really, there isn't. Have you ever had your credit card frozen by mistake? Recently, I was planning a trip to Italy and making hotel reservations; after the second purchase, I received an email alert that my credit card was frozen and in order to continue usage, I would need to call in to verify my identify. The credit card company has software that flags unusual activity, and it deemed my transaction with a hotel in Italy "unusual." Fair enough, right? But that's a classic Type I error. There is no problem, but someone or something feels that there is. In contrast, Type II error is the opposite; there is a relationship, there is a significant activity or indicator, but it is missed or ignored. This would be the equivalent of you not being notified when a thief was running up huge charges on your credit card.

I first became acquainted with these terms during the 1970s when I agreed to participate in a federally funded study in Boston to determine the usefulness of computerized tomographic (CT) scans. CT scans are commonly used now. You probably know someone who's had one done recently, but back then, it was cutting edge technology!

A CT scanner produces cross-sectional images or slices of a person's body by reconstructing a series of X-ray images taken from different angles around the periphery of the body. It was hoped that these detailed pictures of the inside of the body could provide specific diagnoses for people with health problems without having to perform exploratory surgery, and if surgery was necessary it would provide a roadmap that would make the surgery safer and more successful.

Here's how the study worked: All five of us participants in the study agreed to review 100 studies of the head during a four-hour period; there were to be five such sessions. Our task was to decide whether a patient's study was normal or abnormal. If it was abnormal, we were to answer a set of accompanying questions. After the data from our observations had been collected and analyzed, we agreed to be debriefed, at which time we would be told our scores as well as our relative ranking compared to the other participants in the study.

We were being tested on our evaluative skills.

At my debriefing, I assumed that John Sweats, Ph.D., the project director, would give me the percentage that I got right at each session, and then compare my results with the other participants in the project.

True Positives, True Negatives

However, Dr. Sweats' presentation of my test results wasn't as simple as I thought it would be. Instead, he placed my answers within a framework of four categories.[1] Two of these categories would contain correct answers as established by surgery, biopsy, laboratory test or the course of an individual's life.

I could be right because I had correctly identified an abnormal study (true positive), or I could be right because I correctly identified a normal study (true negative).

That's what I wanted to do: identify the abnormal ones and name them abnormal, and identify the normal ones and name them normal.

On the other hand, I might also make two types of errors—the kinds that doctors hate to make.

First, a Type I error would be if I thought there was an abnormality, but there really wasn't one. It's the type of error that a doctor makes when he/she tells a patient that they have a tumor when, in fact, there really isn't one. This type of error would be considered a false positive and lead to a very awkward conversation between the doctor and the patient.

But in looking at these scans, there was also the possibility that I would make another type of mistake, a Type II error. This would happen if I diagnosed a case as normal when it actually wasn't. Perhaps, there was actually a small lesion that I missed or thought was innocuous. I missed the finding. This would be a false negative.

The data from my interpretations were shown to me in a two-by-two (2 x 2) table [2, 3, 4] (Figure 3). These tables categorized my results according to the four types of answers that I described in the previous paragraphs: true positive, true negative, false positive, and false negative.

When I scored a study as *abnormal*, my result would be placed in one of the upper two boxes, depending on whether I was correct or not. If there really was something wrong and I diagnosed it correctly, my answer would be recorded in the true positive box. On the other hand, if I thought that something was amiss but the patient was fine, my answer would be recorded in the false positive box.

When I scored a study as *normal,* my result would be placed in one of the two lower boxes, depending on whether I was right and there was nothing wrong (true negative) or if I was wrong and there actually was a lesion in the study (false negative).

		Proven Abnormal	Proven Normal
Test	Reported Abnormal	True Positive	False Positive (Type I Error)
	Reported Normal	False Negative (Type II Error)	True Negative

Figure 3. Two-by-two table shows the results of the four major types of decisions and where Type I and Type II errors occur. The hypothesis to be tested is located to the left of the table. The proven abnormal and normal at the top of the table are established in medicine by surgery, laboratory test or the course of the individual's disease.

Back on the Farm

Let's reflect on the story of the father and his two sons as we consider the different types of worldviews. The younger brother from our story, being an emotionally-charged FOPE, made a series of Type II errors. He disregarded the information that his father gave him regarding the challenges associated with urban living and insisted that he could take care of himself. Instead, he accepted the fanciful ideas that the caravan merchants used to amuse him while they profitably unloaded their merchandise. He incorrectly felt that he could detect opportunists who would try to take advantage of him. Later, when his money ran out, he sought a variety of jobs for which he felt qualified. Unfortunately, his prospective employers disagreed with him. In other words, his worldview led him to a series of Type II errors that ultimately ruined his life (Figure 4). He's like the doctor who missed the patient's lung tumor; the younger son misjudged reality when he decided to leave home. His version of reality led him to believe that living in the city would give him the pleasure and satisfaction that he felt he couldn't get on the farm. He didn't kill a patient like the doctor who thought everything was fine, but the consequences of his decision did result in losing his fortune, new friends, and self-esteem and even eating food intended for the pigs.

		Proven True	Proven False
Worldview	Exists? (Assumed to Be Real)		
	Doesn't Exist? (Assumed to Be Not Real)	False Negative (Type II Error)	

Figure 4. Type II Error. This is the type of decision errors that FOPEs tend to make.

Ever hear of the "White Swan Fallacy"? For millennia in the Western World, it was assumed that all swans were white because of the collective experience throughout Europe. However, it turned out that in Australia, black swans existed. People with a Type II error mentality are like "people in the old world who were convinced that all swans were white" until black swans were finally discovered in Australia in 1697.[5] They deny the existence of things that are actually true.

With a FOPE worldview, we, like the younger brother, will think primarily of ourselves and how to make our lives exciting and pleasure filled. Even with plenty of information to make good decisions, we too might end up making Type II thinking errors.

Possibly the most destructive effect of the FOPE worldview is that it corrupts the thinking feedback mechanism and leads to dysfunctional thinking (Figures 1 and 2). If FOPEs are to maintain self-esteem in spite of their poor decision outcomes, they have to either debase their feedback system to such an extent that it interprets black as white or restricts their exposure to new experience to limit the number of times they can make false negative decisions. In other words, their worldview makes them either blind to who they really are and the bad decisions they make, or they decrease their exposure to new experiences so they make fewer bad decisions.

The Rule Worldview

On the flip side of the coin, we have people with the ROPE worldview. With their strict paradigm of rules and regulations, ROPEs are more prone to Type I errors. They, like the older brother in our story, tend to see problems when there aren't any. To go back to the CT analogy, the ROPE group would be inclined to make false positive reads on CT scans (Type I error); that is, if they make a mistake, it would be because they think that they've found something wrong when there really wasn't anything wrong.

In response to the ROPE group's desire for stability and respect for authority, ROPE individuals have a tendency to base their relationships on reciprocity, an even exchange of favors summarized in the expression "tit for tat." Figure 5 shows where the ROPE group is located in the 2 x 2 table. It is not surprising that fundamentalist Christians and conservative Muslims, because of their rigidity, have acquired the reputation of being judgmental, grim, and joyless. Furthermore, because in their mind they believe they know the truth, they are resistant to change.

		Exist (Proven True)	Doesn't Exist (Proven Normal)
Worldview	Exists? (Assumed to be real)		False Positive (Type I Error)
	Doesn't Exist? (Assumed to Be Not Real)		

Figure 5. Type 1 Error. This is the type of decision errors that ROPEs tend to make.

A professor at Loma Linda University, Sigve Tonstad in his book *God of Sense and Traditions of Non-Sense*, recounts a story from Russian author Fyodor Dostoyevsky that makes a powerful point about this kind of worldview. I quote Tonstad:

> "His next exhibit is Richard, a Swiss orphan who grew up among the people of Geneva. Little Richard was not allowed to eat from the food that was fed to the animals that he was tending. More than once Dostoyevsky proves

that he knows his Bible. Richard is worse off than the prodigal son in the Gospel of Luke, who was at least allowed to alleviate his hunger with food fed to the swine. When, as an adult, Richard kills a person in a drunken brawl, the attitude of the Christian community changes. Until that point they have given him nothing. Now they descend on him in the prison, urging Richard to accept grace before he faces execution. The Christian mindset and priorities in the account are odd. Geneva, one of the most religious and cultured places in Europe, did not do anything for the orphaned boy when he was in dire need as a child. Why do they take such interest in him when he is found guilty of murder? The apparent change of heart lacks depth, the cruelty of the initial stance now giving way to apparent compassion. When Richard repents and accepts Jesus, the citizens still feel duty bound to execute him. Ivan cannot conceal his scorn. "And so, covered with the kisses of his brothers, brother Richard is dragged up onto the scaffold, laid down on the guillotine, and his head is whacked off in brotherly fashion, forasmuch as grace has descended upon him, too."[6]

This kind of thinking doesn't exist only in religion. Many Germans in World War II committed horrible atrocities. When asked why they did it, the response was simply, "I was only following orders." That's the ROPE view taken to an extreme, but an extreme that, unfortunately, happens more often than we would like to think.

The older brother demonstrated these hard-nosed characteristics when he refused to celebrate his brother's return, while at the same time exuding an aura of moral superiority. One can almost hear him arguing with his father, "This is not how things are supposed to be! We gave him his money, we fulfilled our obligation, so why do we have to take him back? He's broke and he's just come back to get more out of us!"

The MOPE Worldview

For many individuals who have a MOPE worldview, life is purely materialistic, nothing but "atoms and the void." We are just products of what has been called the Selfish Gene Theory. In this theory, humans are mere "survival machines," beings whose sole purpose is to ensure the survival of their genes. Charles Darwin, said zoologist Richard Dawkins (who proposed the theory), got it wrong: evolution isn't to keep the species around.[7] No, evolution's sole purpose is to keep the genes flowing from generation to generation. As a chicken is just an egg's way of making more eggs, humans are just the gene's way of making more genes. According to Dawkins, the genes "are the replicators and we are their survival machines. When we have served our purpose, we are cast aside." From a biological perspective, human are the means, not the ends; the ends are, it seems, more genes.[7]

Adopting a Darwinian philosophy has important consequences since it tends to also lead to Type II errors that assume that nature is all there is (Figure 4). MOPEs are free to construct their own morality. This means they can justify satisfying their primitive needs, regardless of the consequences. It justifies the millions of abortions that take place each year. It ignores the ballooning divorce rate and the increasing number of children growing up in single or unstable families.

This worldview also justifies a preoccupation with money and power since the evolutionary theory justifies"Survival of the Fittest." Many financial leaders in the United States were able to rationalize the collapse of their institutions in 2007–2008 and ask their government for bailout money. This story was told in a fascinating movie, part documentary, called *The Big Short*, in which we see how greed allowed these very rich people to get even richer through sheer callousness and disregard for others. And then, after the collapse, they didn't think it was irrational to award themselves huge bonuses during the restructuring process or to demand that poor, indebted countries that they encouraged to go into debt, pay up.

The MOPEs appear to have more insight in how to achieve social or political success than their FOPE and ROPE counterparts. They realize that they must give up some pleasures and bend some rules if they are to reach their goals and are willing to make Type I and II decision errors as they arbitrarily interpret the situation. Regardless, they justify their behavior by rationalizing that this is what it takes to survive

Science and Authority

Most MOPEs and FOPEs have chosen science as their authority since they have adopted a naturalistic philosophy. They believe that natural causes are sufficient to explain everything that exists. For them, the world is purely materialistic, and, hence, science, which studies the material world (though the word "material" here can refer to forces, fields, waves, whatever), is the only source of truth. This is called "scientism," and it is very prevalent in today's society. MOPEs and FOPEs believe that the information scientists generate can solve the world's problems and create a future utopia.

Alex Rosenberg defined scientism as "the conviction that the methods of science are the only reliable ways to secure knowledge of anything."[8]

As savant Bertrand Russell said in the previous century: "What science cannot tell us, mankind cannot know."[9] The other version of the statement attributed to him is: "What science cannot discover, mankind cannot know."

Or, as John Loftus wrote: "The only thing we can and should trust is the sciences. Science alone produces consistently excellent results that cannot be denied, which are continually retested for validity."[10]

For these individuals and so many more, science is truth and nothing can sway them from that position.

Relationship between Worldview and Lifestyle

Knowing a person's worldview can be incredibly insightful when relating to him/her. When you are aware of just how significant one's worldview is to decision-making, it can help you understand a person's choices or perspectives much more clearly.

For example, during the mid-portion of my career, which coincided with my appointment as head of the neuroradiology department at the Mallinckrodt Institute of Radiology at Washington University in St. Louis, I had the opportunity to see the effect that worldviews had on people.

The neuroradiology department had been having difficulty recruiting faculty and was also in a period of academic stagnation, producing little research to advance the field. I was appointed to solve these problems. Part of my solution was to recruit young neuroradiologists coming out of their fellowships, because I knew that they would bring new energy and enthusiasm to a program that badly need it.

It was in this context that I saw with greater clarity just how much a person's worldview impacts his/her decision-making process.

I found that neuroradiology fellows with a ROPE worldview were nearly impossible to recruit to an academic program. To begin with, they were threatened by the need to publish and the uncertainty of being promoted. Instead, they wanted to live in a community where they felt comfortable and secure, where their parents, teachers, and friends would affirm their success. Furthermore, having a big salary would guarantee that they could pursue a lifestyle superior to that of their parents, former teachers and friends and achieve a higher social status that would further reinforce the idea that they were successful.

I observed many in this group to be ungrateful. They thought they deserved the training that they were receiving because of the hard work and sacrifices they had made throughout medical school and residency. They also tended to be critical, frequently comparing our program with others in regard to salary, workload, and overnight and weekend calls. They regularly used the concept of fairness to try to create situations favorable to themselves. If things didn't go their way, they acted passive-aggressively and could be expected to complain and grumble behind our backs.

Now, here is what is most interesting about this group. Clinically, when the ROPE group made mistakes, they tended to make false positive ones. They thought they saw zebras when there were only wild mustangs. Their overly intense focus on details made them slow workers. I also came to realize that they were poor academic candidates because their conformity hampered their ability to think originally. The ability to think independently and creatively is necessary to advance the field (as measured by research and the subsequent publication of their results) and is the criterion used when people in academia are being considered for promotion.

Despite their materialistic values and self-serving attitudes, I preferred the MOPE candidates to their ROPE counterparts. I know that this sounds cynical, but all I had to determine was how strong the MOPE candidates' need for recognition was and whether they saw that it was in their best interest to be academically productive. It helped that they were more independent and creative and demonstrated higher energy than did the individuals in the ROPE group. If the MOPE candidates had these qualities, I knew they could help the department be what the university wanted it to be.

The decision errors that these MOPE fellows tended to make were related to overconfidence, which in turn led them to *underestimate* the probability of problems. They were prone toward Type II errors.

Not surprisingly, neuroradiology fellow candidates who were in the contemplative zone often wanted to delay their decision if they were offered a position. They wanted just a little bit more time to visit another institution or two, hoping that the new information they gained would help them make the optimal decision. They didn't realize the downside of their worldview. They didn't realize that the world wouldn't stop for them, that there were other well-qualified candidates that were both waiting and willing to take their place. I didn't have much experience with FOPE candidates since few of them had the discipline to make it into medical school.

The HOPE Worldview

In contrast to the ROPE and MOPE groups, there were a few candidates who clearly emanated a HOPE worldview. In their words, in their resumes, in their actions, it was apparent that they would consider the best interests of others when making a decision. Not surprisingly, those candidates were rare.

For a long time I had assumed that utilizing the HOPE worldview was impractical at work. Looking out for the best interests of others was fine when you did volunteer work or on weekends when you were with friends, but on the job? No way!

That was my thinking until I met Jack Thornbury, M.D.,

in the radiology department at the University of Rochester. He singlehandedly convinced me that the HOPE worldview could not only improve my academic productivity but also bring me greater life satisfaction.

When I first met Dr. Thornbury, Magnetic Resonance Imaging (MRI) had just been introduced as a new imaging tool in medicine. Wanting to evaluate this new technology Dr. Thornbury applied and received a coveted National Center for Health Services Research grant. He proposed to test his method of evaluation on patients with multiple sclerosis and low-back pain, as these conditions were among the most common reasons for ordering MRI examinations at that time.

Because Dr. Thornbury was not a neuroradiologist, he invited me to help him recruit patients and, later, to interpret their MR images. During this process I learned how a single person, in this case, Jack, could foster good collaborative relationships by considering the welfare of others, regardless of their background or academic position. He wasn't biased towards scientists or away from physicians; he didn't look down on those without initials in their titles. Through his thoughtful, careful leadership, he was able to create a congenial environment and a productive, well-functioning team.

Jack would encourage people to improve his study based on their unique knowledge and experience. He never took credit for what others had done, but, rather, went out of his way to acknowledge their effort. If an individual in his group wanted to publish, he never insisted on being listed as a co-author even though he had both conceived the idea and raised funds for the study. This is fairly unusual in academic circles where researchers are looking for credit, deserved or not.

Perhaps most important, he was happy to socialize with the entire group, regardless of their academic or social standing. Outings, parties, dinners—Jack was always there, mingling with everyone. His warmth, his care, his selflessness created a feeling of warmth and unity within the group. His HOPE attitude was infectious, and soon other members of his team reflected the same goodwill towards their colleagues.

Before meeting Jack, I had always assumed that this principle of the Golden Rule was not useful at work where one could be trampled on if one practiced it. And, to a certain degree, I was right. He was, in some ways, stepped on. Jack could've received more accolades and been credited with more studies if he had been looking out solely for himself. Some thought he was naïve, but, in fact, the opposite was true. Jack had a profound understanding of the importance of relationships, of a greater purpose in life than just another award or publication.

Additionally, he knew exactly whom he could trust and whom he could not, those safe to let into his inner circle and those who were not. Using his perceptiveness and selflessness, he surrounded himself with a core of people who adopted his worldview—a group who accomplished amazing things not only during the life of the grant but through their subsequent professional careers. He knew how to practice tough love. He could identify individuals who were anxious to take but unable or unwilling to give.[11]

Photo of Jack Thornbury following being awarded the Gold Medal in 2002 by the Association of University Radiologists. Thornbury is on the right. On the left are two of his mentees: Dennis Fryback (center) and Daniel Kido (left).

Relationship between Different Worldviews and Happiness

As human beings, we are all driven by the desire to be happy.

This obsession with happiness is evidenced in blogs, books, TV shows and movies. Pick up the latest popular magazine and count on a self-help article that focuses on how one can attain happiness.

Pop culture presents different formulas for achieving happiness. Some focus on financial wealth; others push physical pleasure and well-being; others a peaceful life free of conflict. Few suggest pursing long-lasting, meaningful relationships. These formulas, the resulting types of happiness and the outcomes they produce can be grouped by worldview (Table 1).

Worldviews	Motivation	Happiness	Outcome
FOPE	Self	Physical pleasure; immediate happiness	Impatient, impulsive
ROPE	Rules	Mental satisfaction associated with being right; delayed happiness	Rigid, critical, overly concerned with fairness
MOPE	Self/Rules	Status, money, power; temporary happiness	Arrogant, competitive, greedy
HOPE	Others	Satisfaction from meaningful relationships; lasting happiness	Patient, kind, grateful, optimistic

Table 1. Different worldviews and their relationship to various types of motivation, happiness (well-being), and outcome.

Summary

Peter Drucker, a well-known leadership and management expert, described three types of sports teams as a metaphor for organizations: football, baseball, and tennis doubles.[12] Football players must follow the coach's rules and function as a unit if they are to be successful. To replace a member of the football team without disrupting its efficiency is difficult. Professional football players who put their self-interest first are unpopular and are usually dropped or traded from their teams. Finally, football teams are totally dependent on the coach's preparation for the game and the plays he calls.

In contrast, baseball teams are a collection of individuals who gather to play a common game but who, for the most part, perform separately and can be judged individually. Players on baseball teams can be easily replaced with little disruption to the team's performance. Although baseball teams need a coach to tell them where they are to play and when they are going to bat, the coach has less impact on the players during the game than does the football coach.

The tennis doubles team is different from the other two teams because it does not have a coach directing the game. Its members must learn to think for themselves and cooperate with one another without outside supervision during the game.

Drucker argues that leaders may find it useful for their organizations to function as different types of teams in different situations. However, he asserts that the tennis-doubles mentality is the most useful if an organization wants to achieve long-term success.

I believe this analogy can be extended to the function of worldviews as well. One could argue that football players roughly correspond to individuals with a ROPE worldview. They need outside direction or a pattern that ties them together in order to function well. Their dependency on rules, on their coach, rings true with ROPE.

Baseball players, on the other hand, can be likened to those with either the FOPE or MOPE worldview. They excel at functioning on their own. They're there to play together, but each player is looking out for himself.

Tennis-doubles players, in contrast, can be compared to those with a HOPE worldview, because each partner must not only be critical of his or her own skills but also choose to complement their partner's skills if they are to be a successful team. This means that they will have to give up their feeling of individual entitlement if they expect to win and experience the mutual happiness they both desire.

While on the field, all three types of teams can achieve success. In real life, the same can be true but in varying degrees. The ROPE group (football players) and the FOPE/ MOPE group (baseball players) may achieve their goals, but their happiness will be sporadic, dependent on always reaching the next success or high. Failures can be devastating to these groups, since it means that they are not as special as they thought they were or that the activities that gave their life meaning may be meaningless.

In contrast, those who are like tennis-doubles players, who are willing to do what's best for their partners, will likely have the greatest degree of contentment in the long run. This is because their happiness is based on a meaningful relationship with each other and the satisfaction of living for something bigger than their own self-interest. Adapting to one another's strengths and weaknesses and growing together results in their continuing satisfaction. Failure points out their need to critically evaluate their skills and practice to improve them, providing opportunities to develop a deeper relationship.

Perhaps even better than the tennis-doubles analogy is Drucker's reference to jazz groups. The jazz musicians come together and must first learn one another's strengths, weaknesses, and styles. However, their goal is to function as a group that can make more interesting and beautiful music than they could create on their own. Each musician allows all the others to flourish in their talent, and together they become a harmonized unit that wows audiences. I believe that the research group Jack created worked like a jazz group.

Our free will allows us the ability to choose a worldview. While we may not be in control of many other aspects of our lives, we do have control over this. And it is up to us to decide which worldview we believe will lead to the best, most positive, and long-lasting outcomes.

chapter 3

Making Sure Your Choices (Decisions) Are Better Than Chance

On a beautiful day in August 1945, Kenshi Hirata, a newly married young man, was working in a Mitsubishi plant in Hiroshima, Japan.[1] That afternoon, he glanced out the factory window and saw what he later described as the most beautiful lightning flash he had ever seen. Seconds later, the entire plant felt as if it were rising off the ground and then dropped. Kenshi found himself surrounded by rubble and debris from the collapsed building, yet amazingly he was unhurt. Chaos ensued as cries from the other workers echoed around him. Men stumbled to their feet, clothes bloodied and covered with dust.

Kenshi emerged from the building that had collapsed into a world on fire. Driven by thoughts of his wife, he staggered home. Kenshi uttered a low moan as he turned the corner to his driveway. Nothing was left standing. Still, he entered the remains of his home and pawed frantically through the wreckage. And there, buried under the kitchen ceiling, Kenshi found the bones and ashes of his beloved young wife.

Functioning on nothing more than adrenaline and desperation, Kenshi collected her remains and placed them in a small box, determined to return her to her parents. He walked to the barely operating train station and caught the last train out.

The city he was going to?

Nagasaki.

A few days later, the second atomic bomb exploded.

And poor Kenshi Hirata was there!

Same white flash. Same immediate destruction.

Kenshi cried out as the "beautiful light" ripped open his in-laws' home, crushing their furniture and belongings, including the box with his wife's remains. He miraculously survived the second explosion.

Talk about being a victim of forces beyond his control! Through no fault of his own, he was one of the few people in all history to be nuked, not just once but twice, and survive!

Of course, you don't have to be the victim of an atomic bomb explosion to feel yourself at the mercy of forces greater than yourself. Tsunamis, earthquakes, hurricanes, and other natural disasters have destroyed countless families' lives, swallowing up all their worldly possessions and leaving them without food or shelter in the blink of an eye.

The effects of man-made catastrophes can be equally destructive. A few bad loans made on Wall Street and thousands of jobs are lost throughout the United States. The finance minister in England signs a resolution and a business in Myanmar goes under. A civil war in Syria turns its residents into refugees, fleeing for their lives.

Missed stop signs, freak electrical fires, undiagnosed genetic conditions—these are all random, unforeseeable circumstances that can dramatically change our lives.

We all know that our lives are greatly impacted by forces that we cannot control. We are conceived as the result of choices we didn't make, we are born to parents whom we didn't choose, and our earliest years (the most important ones) unfold in an environment over which we have no say.

But while there are factors in our lives that we cannot control, I prefer to spend my time and energy focusing on the ones that we can control. The choices we do have and the decisions we can make is what this book is about.

Models

Models are symbols or representations that stand for something else. We see models in lots of different places. Statues, ancient or modern, are models of the people or things that they were created to represent. Ancient Greek sculptors depicted the perfect human body based on proportion and balance. Paintings can also be symbols for a reality that painters want to depict; similarly, maps are also models, but of the actual world we live in. There's a famous photo of Adolph Hitler taken from the last days of World War II that shows him studying a model that he hoped would be the New Berlin, the future capital of the world.

Science also works with models, perhaps more than most people realize. For example, one of the most common models is the atomic model—the nucleus of the atom surrounded by electrons. It represents what we think is the atomic structure. There are also things such as the Plate Tectonic Model, the evolutionary model, and even models concerning one of the most elusive things in the known world—the light model.

In all these cases, the models represent, to some degree, something from the physical world. But the worldview models that I have presented so far in this book are different; they deal with an abstract concept. A worldview is an idea, a mental construct—and I have been presenting various illustrations that reflect these worldviews and the ideas that they represent.

But while ideas are just a representation of something abstract, they, too, can have profound consequences since the type of worldview model we hold greatly impacts our decisions, which, in turn, ultimately determine our destiny.

But how closely does this idea, this worldview, mirror actual reality? I remember the first time I watched a 3-D film. Walking into the theater, I was handed a pair of plastic glasses to wear during the movie. The glasses seemed ineffective at first; all the PR touting 3-D animation as the latest and greatest in visual effects seemed like just a marketing ploy: I felt duped. But then the movie began and I was blown away! The villains were literally jumping off the screen at me, and I even caught myself ducking once or twice when debris seemed to be flying at me. How was this happening? What were these flimsy pieces of plastic doing to my vision? I couldn't stop playing with the glasses; I'd push them up for a split second and then bring them back down over my eyes, checking and re-checking what reality was versus what I was seeing through the glasses.

I feel like we need to do the same thing when it comes to the worldview we hold. We should flip up our glasses every once in a while to determine if our perception of reality is actually what's out there.

Sensitivity and Specificity

In the previous chapter, I used a 2 x 2 table to show that there are four major categories of decisions (models) that correspond to the four groups of decision-makers (ROPE, FOPE, MOPE, and HOPE). I attempted to show why three of these groups have a greater propensity to make decision errors because of how their worldview distorts their view of reality.

I hypothesized that two of these groups, the FOPE and ROPE groups, are prone to systematic errors—false negative for FOPE and false positive for the ROPE. In other words, ROPEs tend to find something wrong when there's nothing wrong, while the FOPEs think everything is fine when things actually aren't. ROPEs tend to finds faults, errors, and problems when there are none, and FOPEs, because they focus on themselves, miss problems that stare them right in the face. MOPEs are willing to make both types of errors when they think it will be advantageous to them.

None of these groups is particularly good at making decisions because of their tendency to make systematic errors. It's as if their 3-D glasses are broken. If their glasses distort reality, how can we expect them to have an accurate picture of what is truly happening? How can we expect them to make consistently good decisions?

In the previous chapter, I recounted my participation in a study where my accuracy in reading CT scans of the brain was evaluated by Dr. Sweats. Remember how he placed my results in a 2 x 2 table in order to determine whether or not I could detect an abnormality and accurately identify it (true positive) or whether or not I could correctly identify normal (true negative).

The words *sensitivity* and *specificity* are used to describe the percentage of times I correctly identified items in each category.[2,3]

Sensitivity is the proportion of time I said something was abnormal and it was, actually, abnormal. In other words, I was sensitive to the reality of the problem. I got it right. *Specificity*, in contrast, is the proportion of time I said something was normal and it turned out to be normal. I could specifically see that things were all right when they were.

I introduce the concepts of "sensitivity" and "specificity" to illustrate how numerical data taken from a 2 x 2 table can be transferred onto a graph that has ssensitivity and specificity as coordinates (Figure 6).

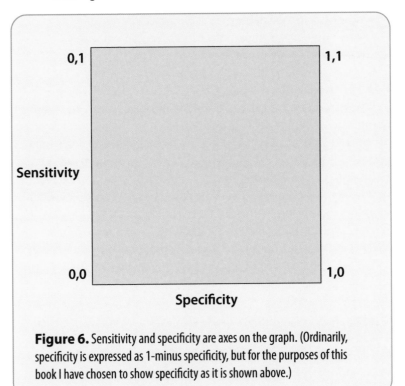

Figure 6. Sensitivity and specificity are axes on the graph. (Ordinarily, specificity is expressed as 1-minus specificity, but for the purposes of this book I have chosen to show specificity as it is shown above.)

Dr. Sweats took data from each of my sessions and placed them in a 2x 2 table, calculated my sensitivity and specificity and then plotted them on a graph, similar to Figure 6, to determine how accurately I identified abnormal and normal CT scans. This allowed him to visually compare my results from session to session and also my results with the other participants in the study. He did this because he realized that by visually displaying the data he had collected it would be easier for him to detect a pattern or patterns from which he could make generalizations about the usefulness of CT scanners.

Just as Dr. Sweats broke down my accuracy into its components and then displayed them on a graph, so, too, can worldviews be broken down into its two major components and plotted. For this concept, however, we will use two different words: reason and emotion.

How often do we make a decision based on reason?
How often do we make a decision based on emotion?
How often do we use both?

Reason and Emotion

Since antiquity it has been understood that reason and emotion are the major components in human decision-making and that they are pitted against each other. Plato used the images of a charioteer with two horses to show the struggle between emotion and reason in human beings. Philosophers, psychologists, ethicists, and even neuroscientists continue to wrestle with the relationship between emotion and reason. Some call these two components nature/nurture while others label this dichotomy "heart" and "mind." Whatever the label, once these two components of worldviews are identified, they can be put as axes on a graph (Figures 7A).

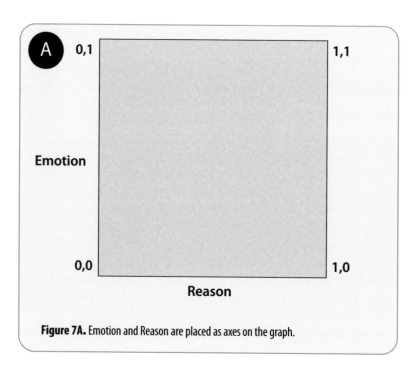

Figure 7A. Emotion and Reason are placed as axes on the graph.

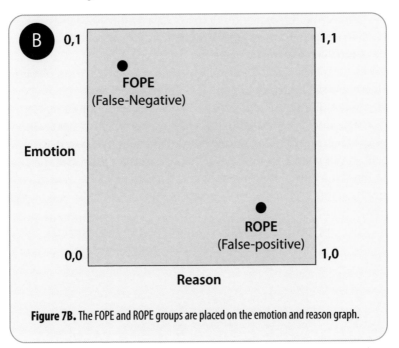

Figure 7B. The FOPE and ROPE groups are placed on the emotion and reason graph.

I thought it might be useful to place the FOPE and ROPE worldviews on the emotion/reason graph to see where they might fall (Figure 7B). Of course, there are various contexts and experiences, factors and situations that make it impossible to speak specifically to every individual and his/her worldview. However, I think it's helpful to map it out like this, even in general terms, to more easily look for relationships.

I postulate that a typical ROPE person makes decisions based on 80 percent reason and 20 percent emotion. This trade-off of one factor for another is seen again and again in the scientific world. Following this reasoning, an increase in the emotional value of the ROPE person is accompanied by a decrease in reason, which then would result in his/her "dot" moving closer to the contemplative zone that is located mid-way between the ROPE and FOPE groups (Figure 8).

A FOPE thinker is roughly the opposite. He/she might make decisions based largely on emotions (80 percent) and less on reason (20 percent).

There is an important thing to note about these observations. No one is 100 percent of any worldview and therefore might occasionally make uncharacteristic decisions. A diabetic ROPE, for instance, who might generally be a no-nonsense type of person ruled by strict precepts, can still be swayed by the dessert bar where he's dining. He remembers that his doctor told him to keep his sugar intake low, but still, that dark chocolate cheesecake with peanut butter swirls is shouting his name and he yields to its siren call. In that moment, his appetite (emotion) rules his reason.

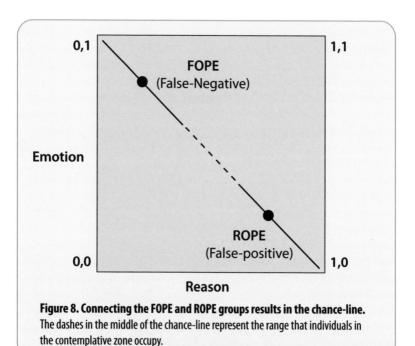

Figure 8. Connecting the FOPE and ROPE groups results in the chance-line. The dashes in the middle of the chance-line represent the range that individuals in the contemplative zone occupy.

The second thing to note is that a straight line can be drawn through the two worldview positions (Figure 8). In the world of statistics a straight line through the two worldviews means they must share at least one underlying characteristic. I recently found some fascinating data that underlines this point. This research compared certain issues in the lifestyles of Christians and non-Christians. I assumed that Christians tend to be, as a whole, more

ROPE-oriented, while non-Christians might hold a more FOPE or MOPE worldview. One might also hypothesize that these opposing worldviews would result in different outcomes. However, as you can see in Table 2, there is actually little difference in behavior or satisfaction with life between the two groups, although in many ways they believe, behave and live differently from each other.

	Christians (ROPE)	Non-Christians (FOPE/MOPE)
Donated money to charity in the last month	47%	48%
Attended a community meeting in the past year	37%	43%
Took drugs for depression	7%	8%
Satisfied with life	69%	68%

Table 2. Comparison of the lifestyles and life satisfaction of Christians and Non-Christians.[4]

The Chance-Line

As I said, because we can draw a straight line between the FOPE and ROPE worldviews, there must be at least one characteristic that they share. Although the FOPE and ROPE groups believe and live differently, an especially important characteristic they share is their lack of accuracy in making decisions because they exist along a line mid-way between the 0.0 and 1,1 points called the chance-line. People who live along this line, depicted in Figure 8, regardless of their location on the line, have only about a 50:50 chance (random outcome) of making decisions that turn out the way that they planned. Again, they might as well flip a coin in making their life's important decisions. Flipping a quarter, for example, supports the probability of heads coming up as 50:50. That's great for deciding which team receives the football in a football game, but that's hardly the way to make life-changing decisions.

Referee flipping a coin at a football game. Asa Nemoto

Decision-makers who are located closer to the 0/0 point have less than a 50:50 chance of achieving a predicted outcome. On the other hand, the closer they inch towards the 1/1 point, the higher the probability they have of obtaining their expected outcome. The graph in Figure 8 shows the range of outcomes that can occur in any given situation.

So, which of these worldviews results in the best outcomes?

From the graph in Figure 8, decisions made by the ROPE and FOPE worldviews—when they are located in the region of the 50:50 line—are all equally random and due to chance. Not a particularly great way to make important life decisions, is it? Imagine deciding on whom to marry by flipping a coin?

Heads, we get married; tails, we don't.

Or for a career path? Heads, I study physical therapy; tails, I study auto mechanics.

The patterned region on the graph in Figure 9 shows the region occupied by those with FOPE, ROPE, and MOPE worldviews as well as those in the contemplative zone. Their decisions become worse as they approaches the 0/0 area. Hitler, as he aged descended towards the 0/0 point because he continued to corrupt his feedback mechanism and thus degraded his ability to see reality.

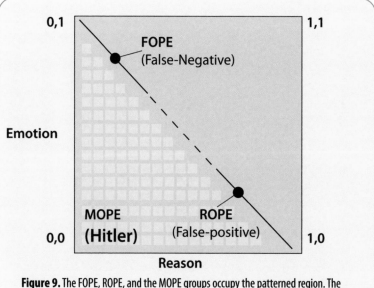

Figure 9. The FOPE, ROPE, and the MOPE groups occupy the patterned region. The dashes in the chance-line represent the Contemplative group. Hitler anchors the 0/0 point.

Surely, there must be a better way to make decisions. And there is. It's called the HOPE worldview.

The Hope Worldview

Individuals with a HOPE worldview occupy the patterned area to the right of the chance line and up to the 1/1 point, where decisions are more likely to result in good outcomes (Figure 10).

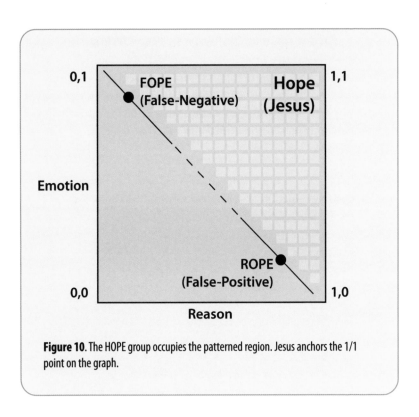

Figure 10. The HOPE group occupies the patterned region. Jesus anchors the 1/1 point on the graph.

And therein lies the answer to our question. If we want to have a better chance of having optimal outcomes with our decisions, the answer is to adopt the HOPE worldview.

The best example of an individual who embodied the HOPE worldview is Jesus of Nazareth, the central figure in the New Testament Bible. Jesus anchors the 1/1 point on the graph because he consistently made good decisions. He had a worldview that positively utilized feelings and rules. He had a perfectly functioning feedback loop that gave him an unusually accurate perception of reality. He used the freedom his perception of reality gave him to liberate himself from social and political considerations when helping those with either physical or spiritual needs.

Regardless of one's religious views, most people are impressed by the beauty and power of Jesus's teachings and character. Albert Einstein, certainly not a Christian, said this about Jesus:

> "No one can read the Gospels without feeling the actual presence of Jesus. His personality pulsates in every word. No myth is filled with such life. How different, for instance, is the impression which we receive from an account of legendary heroes of antiquity like Theseus. Heroes of his type lack the authentic vitality of Jesus."[5]

Jesus fits into the upper right-hand corner of the graph (Figure 10). He positively blends reason and emotion into an altruistic worldview. He was wise and emotionally mature because he was not blinded by self-interest. Instead his life was focused on developing meaningful relationships with those whom he came to serve. As he said: "For even the Son of Man did not come to be served, but to serve, and to give His life a ransom for many."[6] Every aspect of his life could be defined by self-renunciation, self-abnegation, all for the good of others. That's how he lived and that's how he taught others to live.

These characteristics allowed him to value all people regardless of their social or economic standing, gender, race, or political views. Moreover, he was likable and winsome: even children were drawn to him, and it is clear that he enjoyed them, perhaps because of their innocence and spontaneity.

Summary
The story of Kenshi Hirata, twice nuked, reveals to some degree what we all know: there are forces out there that we cannot control.

At the same time, we also know that we do have the power of choice over many things. And our choices, more than anything else, determine our future and the kind of life we will live. This is why I believe that choosing the right worldview is so incredibly important.

Our worldview, the "glasses" that we have on, significantly impacts the kind of decisions we make. So what glasses should we wear? Which glasses provide us with the clearest vision of reality and allow us to make the best decisions? No question: the HOPE worldview!

chapter 4

The Hope Group versus the Groups Along or Beneath the Chance-Line

"The Enormous Radio," by John Cheever, is a short story about a typical married couple with two young children living in a twelfth-floor apartment in Manhattan.[1]

"Jim and Irene Westcott were the kind of people who seem to strike that satisfactory average of income, endeavor, and respectability that is reached by the statistical reports in college alumni bulletins."

They also, he wrote, "went to the theatre an average of 10.3 times a year."

Sounds like ROPE, doesn't it?

One day Jim brought home a radio housed in a large wooden box, the kind that exists only in museums today. Much to their surprise, the new radio allowed them to listen in on others in their building. "Those must be the Fullers in 11-E," Irene said. "I knew they were giving a party this afternoon. I saw her in the liquor store. Isn't this too divine? Try something else. See if you can get those people in 18-C."

Over time, though, the wooden box and its "news" disturbed Irene. Jim came home one day and found her upset over the fighting, the dysfunction, the dishonesty, and the battles over money and other things that she heard all day over the radio. When he angrily told her to stop listening, she begged him not to fight with her and to affirm that they were happy and that their lives weren't as sordid and messed up as the others in the building. After assuring her they were different, Irene calmed down, and Jim got the radio fixed so that only music came from it.

A few weeks later, Jim and Irene did get into an argument over money. Irene shushed him quickly, warning him that others would hear. "Who?" he asked, confused. "The Radio," she responded impatiently. He protested that the radio had been fixed and wouldn't pick up their conversations anyway; and besides, he added indignantly, he wouldn't care if it did. Jim continued his attack, accusing Irene of being hypocritical. "You stole your mother's jewelry before they probated her will. You never gave your sister a cent of that money that was intended for her—not even when she needed it. You made Grace Howland's life miserable, and where was all your piety and your virtue when you went to that abortionist? I'll never forget how cold you were. You packed your bag and went off to have that child murdered as if you were going to Nassau."

Cheever ends it like this:

> "Irene stood for a minute before the hideous cabinet, disgraced and sickened, but she held her hand on the switch hoping that the instrument might speak to her kindly. . . . Jim continued to shout at her from the door. The voice on the radio was suave and non-committal. 'An early-morning railroad disaster in Tokyo,' the loudspeaker said, 'killed twenty-nine people. A fire in a Catholic hospital that cares for blind children near Buffalo was extinguished early this morning by nuns. The temperature is forty-seven. The humidity is eighty-nine.'"

Cheever makes a statement about the domestic abjection of the American lifestyle in the 1950s. I think we can find FOPE, ROPE and MOPE in his story since all these worldviews are motivated by self-interest and result in poor outcomes. In Table 3, we can see the effects of FOPE, ROPE and MOPE worldviews on the Cheever's family and how they radically contrast with the HOPE worldview.

	FOPE/ROPE/MOPE	HOPE
Motivation	Self	Others
Growth	Illusionary/selfish growth	Altruistic growth
Decision Results	Chance or worse	Better than chance
Social interactions	Takers/watchers	Givers (know when to use tough love)
Satisfaction with life	Lonely/depressed	Connected and content

Table 3. Comparison of the FOPE/ROPE/MOPE groups located along or beneath the chance-line with the HOPE group.

Differences Between the Groups Along or Beneath the Chance-Line and the HOPE Group

As summarized in Table 3, there are clear differences between those with the HOPE worldview and the groups along or beneath the chance-line.

The motivation in decision-making for the groups on or below the chance-line is that they look out for themselves while pursuing happiness: they wish for an exciting, carefree life; a comfortable, leisure-filled life; or a life where they have status and power. Young ROPEs pursue education to acquire marketable skills that they anticipate will give them the financial means to achieve security, respectability, and the time to pursue their concept of happiness. This might include joining the right country club or church, placing their children in a private school to demonstrate that they have made it, or take exotic vacations so that they can tell their friends about it. Despite their seeming success, most of them are not totally content.

FOPEs are also chasing happiness in their own way. An extreme example of this is Latrell Sprewell, a former basketball player. In 1992 he was a first-round draft pick by the basketball team in the San Francisco Bay area. He was an immediate success and eventually even became an all-star. He was hot tempered and didn't like criticism. One day during practice his coach yelled at him to make crisper passes. When his coach approached him, Sprewell threatened to kill him and actually began choking him. He was suspended for the remainder of the season.

The next season Sprewell successfully played for New York and then later for Minnesota. In 2005, while playing for Minnesota, he was offered a $21 million three-year extension. He publicly expressed his outrage at that offer, declaring, "I have a family to feed." Within two years he was out of the league, had left his family, and was broke.

I wonder whether Sprewell ever realized that his ideas about success and happiness weren't producing the results he had hoped for, as the Westcotts eventually did. In fact, the more the people on or below the chance-line pursue happiness, the more likely those around them will observe their selfishness and avoid them.

Finally, MOPEs who utilize both FOPE and ROPE values when they think its advantageous are also chasing happiness. They justify their selfish attitude and actions by telling themselves it's just human nature. They may even take pride in their ability to take advantage of others since they believe it's a "dog eat dog" world where only the fittest survive. With this philosophy they can also justify intimidating and coercing others when it's important for them to get their way. Unfortunately, with this attitude it is difficult for MOPEs to develop meaningful relationships with others.

Human Loneliness

Those most desperate to find happiness, it seems, are also the most likely to be the loneliest. Ronald Rolheiser has suggested that the pursuit of happiness may really be an attempt to escape loneliness.[2] As our society has evolved technologically, it has also become more overt in seeking happiness, and in the process it has become more uncivil and disconnected.

Robert Putnam noted in *Bowling Alone*: ". . . our evidence also suggests that across a very wide range of activities, the last several decades have witnessed a striking diminution of regular contacts with our friends and neighbors."[3]

He illustrates this by pointing out that although bowling, the most popular competitive sport in the United States, experienced a 10 percent growth in players between 1980 and 1993, the number of bowlers participating in leagues fell by 40 percent. Putnam observed similar decreasing trends in local community participation (political campaigns, parent-teacher associations, and a variety of local clubs and organizations), church attendance, and social interactions at work and home. The success of social media networks such as Facebook can probably be explained by the human need for social interaction no matter how diluted or artificial it may be. However, in spite of increased connectivity through media, people have become more detached and lonely.

The Death of Joyce Vincent

The headline in the *London Sun* read: "Woman dead in flat for three years: skeleton of Joyce found on sofa with telly still on."

Dead for three years in a London apartment, and no one missed her? No one knew? No one called to check on her? No one wondered where she was? Dead on the sofa with the television still on—after three years! How could this happen, especially in a day of almost limitless communication? People obviously knew her, because she had a few Christmas presents lying around. Yet somehow, no one noted her absence.

When the story first broke in 2006, it made international news. People in London, a city of eight million, asked themselves hard questions about "the lack of community spirit in the UK."

Carol Morley, a writer and director, wrote about this unfortunate story after she picked up a discarded newspaper in a London subway and read about Joyce Vincent.[4] She wrote: "The image of the television flickering over her decomposing body haunted me as I got off the train onto the crowded platform. In a city like London how could someone's absence go unnoticed for so long? Who was Joyce Vincent? What was she like? How could she have been forgotten?"[5]

According to Morley, after the initial splash and the social media outcry, the story of Joyce Vincent eventually vanished. And yet the question remained: How could this beautiful young woman, a very talented singer, known as "the life of the party," die at age 38 and then simply vanish from the minds of all those who knew her?

Along, Beneath and Above the Chance-Line

Though Joyce Vincent's case may be an extreme example, it does point out the current reality of human alienation and human loneliness. Isolation and loneliness are some of the consequences of making a life full of bad decisions. For FOPEs it's moving closer to the 0,1 point. For ROPEs it is moving closer to the 1,0 point. FOPE and MOPE people do not seem to realize that their selfishness will alienate others and contribute to their loneliness. This loneliness can lead to depression and then possibly even to despair. [6, 7, 8]

The ROPEs also alienate people but it's by their rigidness, criticalness, cynicism, and their distortion of reality. Jim and Irene Westcott illustrate how their worldviews negatively affected their interpersonal relationship, as well as those with their neighbors. If the gap between who ROPEs think they should be and who they really are becomes too great, they may begin to experience anxiety, compulsions and obsessions that can lead to depression.

How ironic: the more individuals on or below the chance line strive for what they think will make them happy, the unhappier they become.

In contrast, those with the HOPE mentality will, as they move farther and farther away from the chance-line and closer to the 1/1 point in Figure 10, make better and better decisions and build an increasingly stronger social network because of their interest in and consideration of others. As they grow they will become more capable of forming intimate, meaningful relationships because of their willingness to confront their fears and shortcomings. In this process they will become more compassionate and content.

In other words, the more the HOPEs work for the happiness of others, the more contentment they experience. In contrast, the more selfish those on and below the chance-line become, and the more they do things that they think will make them happy, the more misery they experience.

Illusionary Growth

Another important difference between the chance-line groups and the HOPE group is shown in Table 3, and that is growth. FOPEs who move closer and closer to the 0,1 point and are more and more desirous of pleasurable experiences become more

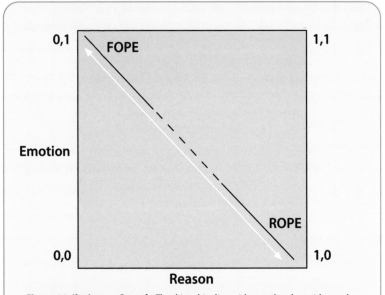

Figure 11. Ilusionary Growth. The thin white line with arrowheads at either end, paralleling the chance-line, shows that what the FOPE and ROPE groups perceive as growth is actually just exploration of a different part of the same line.

egotistical, more self-serving and more uninhibited. They are susceptible to addictions especially if they had experienced early emotional trauma or lived in an addictive environment. Psychiatrist Scott Peck points out that when impulsive, self-serving FOPEs positively engage in psychotherapy, they become more conforming and disciplined.[9] In the process, they may even find religion and join a church, especially a conservative one that envisions God as a transcendent judge. Growth for these people is moving toward a more ROPE-centric portion of the chance-line. Although they appear and behave differently, they will only have moved to a different position along the chance-line (Figure 11). They will not have experienced significant growth since they are still located on the same chance-line and have the same motivation and thinking mode. Eventually they will experience a different kind of selfish misery; that's all.

Conversely, Dr. Peck notes that religious, rigid, conforming

ROPE individuals who are involved in successful therapy frequently become nominal Christians, agnostics, or atheists, and in the process either move toward the less-structured FOPE life style or down towards the MOPEs. Thus, growth for both these groups is simply exploring a different part of the chance-line or the region below the line without ever escaping it and entering the HOPE region. These groups are experiencing either illusionary or selfish growth. When both these groups were passing through the contemplative zone, they had the opportunity to explore the HOPE worldview but chose to just explore another portion of the chance-line or the area beneath the line because this did not require changing their underlying motivation.

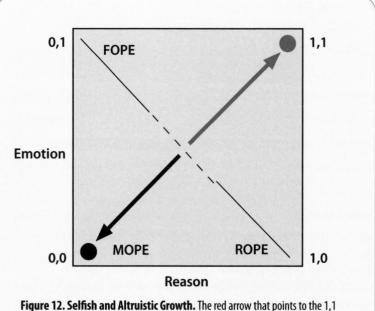

Figure 12. Selfish and Altruistic Growth. The red arrow that points to the 1,1 point represents altrustic growth that is experienced by the HOPE group. The black arrow that points to the 0,0 point represents selfish growth that is experienced by the MOPE group.

Selfish Growth

MOPEs' growth, as they move towards the 0,0 point, is deceptive (Figure 12). Initially, the energy and focus they exhibit makes them the "go getters" that society rewards. Their philosophy of "survival of the fittest" appears to be paying off. Later, as these individuals move closer to the 0,0 point and have acquired more influence /power, they are prone to utilizing intimidation, coercion or force to get their way. In the process meaningful relationships with others deteriorate.

If successful MOPEs have children, they may instill in their children a feeling that they are special and possibly even superior to others because that's how they feel about themselves. Their mother or perhaps a nanny caters to their whims. Their mother feels they can do no wrong. Their father makes up for his absence by lavishing them with gifts. When their children don't get high grades, they confront their teachers. When their children need a couple more days to finish a term paper, they call the teacher for them. In other words, these parents shelter their children from the discomforts of life and don't allow them to fail. As a result their children become emotionally fragile and lack resilience. Some of these children may become FOPEs.

Setbacks are devastating to these children because these incidents indicate that they may not be as special as they were led to think. When something bad happens, it's always someone else's fault, not theirs. In the process, their feedback system becomes dysfunctional, paralleling those of their parents. If they can't excuse themselves, they may become depressed, "tormenting themselves with ideas that the setbacks meant they were incompetent or unworthy."[10] Unfortunately, many in this group dismiss the idea of having to expend undue effort to correct a shortcoming; after all, wouldn't that be an admission that they are not special? As a result they do not develop grit, and many of them fail when they go to college where their parents can no longer protect them.[11]

Altruistic Growth

And what of the HOPE thinkers? Where do they stand in all this?

People with a HOPE mentality have a mindset that their basic abilities and personality traits can be improved through effort and experience. They know that they have to work if they expect to grow (Figure 12). They are open to accurate, unflattering assessments of their performance since they have adopted a humble, teachable spirit. They see failure as a stepping stone to success and new challenges as opportunities to stretch themselves. If these challenges are in line with their interests, they are relentless in working to understand the field and will eventually become experts. They are excited about improving their skills because they realize that they will be more capable of helping others. As their knowledge and skills improve, they will acknowledge what they owe to others. Thus, they develop close relationships with those individuals who have helped them to grow.

As the HOPE individuals move away from the chance-line toward the 1/1 point, they develop altruistically. They will also become more compassionate. Even when they disagree with their colleagues or friends, they will be courteous and respectful because they value others. They realize that meaningful interactions with others will help them grow. This makes me think of some words by the apostle Paul in the *New Testament Bible*, which, even outside a religious context, powerfully reveals the way a HOPE person lives. Paul writes: "Let nothing be done through selfish ambition or conceit, but in lowliness of mind let each esteem others better than himself. Let each of you look out not only for his own interests, but also for the interests of others."[12]

That's the essence of a HOPE view, and people with this worldview are inevitably going to be happier and more fulfilled than those who remain on or below the chance line. As HOPE people move farther and farther away from the chance-line and closer to the 1/1 point, their grasp of reality improves and becomes less distorted by bias. They think less of themselves and more of others. They desire personal freedom to pursue their altruistic interests. In the process, they become more disciplined mentally, socially, and physically. Their thinking allows them to connect, cooperate, and become more creative, and thus they become better decision-makers. The altruistic projects they participate in give them a feeling of purpose, which, in turn, results in self-contentment.

Simply put, HOPEs are happiest when thinking of and helping others.

Politicians such as Abraham Lincoln and Nelson Mandela, humanitarians such as William Wilberforce and Mother Theresa, spiritual leaders such as the Dalai Lama and Desmond Tutu, authors such as Vaclav Havel and Aleksandr Solzhenitsyn and economists such as Peter Drucker and Edward Deming—these well-known figures embody the HOPE worldview. They have all focused on the well-being of others and, as a result, have brought meaning and purpose to their own lives and the lives of others.

Consider Nelson Mandela, who spent 27 years in prison because of his anti-apartheid activities. When he was released, he did not focus on revenge, but instead, focused on creating a new society where black and white people work together.[13] He used forgiveness as an effective tool in his "reconciliation program." He was creative and flexible enough to use the national rugby team, previously a symbol of white power, to help him draw whites and blacks together. (This point is beautifully illustrated in the movie *Invictus*, starring Morgan Freeman as Mandela and Matt Damon as the captain of the rugby team.)

In his economic models, leadership guru Peter Drucker puts a high value on people.[14] He pointed out that in advanced, knowledge-driven societies, humans become the most important capital. He asserts that employees with knowledge, because of their mobility, must be treasured as valuable assets; corporations that do not realize this will lose their competitive edge.

In his book *Good to Great*, Jim Collins, a protege of Drucker, contrasts good and great leaders. He observes that great leaders are modest, shunning the public adulation that self-centered individuals crave.[15] These leaders aren't afraid to surround themselves with exceptional executives who aid them in defining their goals and unwaveringly pursuing them. And because such leaders surround themselves with exceptional colleagues, succession is not a problem; in fact, the company may go on to even greater success when a protégé takes over.

The HOPE leaders that Collins describes are sought after more today than ever before because of their potential to grow. In the past, it was enough to be intelligent, experienced, and competent, but in today's world of volatility, uncertainty, complexity and ambiguity, leaders must have the potential to learn new skills and adapt to an ever-changing environment.[16]

In other words, leaders with a HOPE worldview will be in greater demand than ever before.

The Meaning of Life

A young writer recalled a week spent with the Dalai Lama in Santa Fe during the mid-80s as his press secretary.[17] During that time the Dalai Lama made a special request to visit the local ski resort. On the way up on the chairlift, he was interested in the skiers, since he had never seen skiing before, but he was especially enthusiastic about the beauty of the mountains. The view made him wistful and reminded him of his home in Tibet.

After riding the chairlift back down the mountain, they had cookies and hot chocolate at the lodge. The Dalai Lama talked to the skiers in the lodge and was amazed to learn that even handicapped one-legged individuals could ski. As the visit was coming to an end, a young waitress with tangled, blond hair and a beaded headband began clearing the tables around the Dalai Lama. She stopped to listen to the conversation and finally sat down, abandoning her work. At the first pause, she spoke to the Dalai Lama.

"You didn't like your cookie?"

"Not hungry, thank you."

"Can I, um, ask a question?"

"Please."

She spoke with complete seriousness.

"What is the meaning of life?"

During the writer's entire week with the Dalai Lama, every conceivable question had been asked except this one, the really big question. There was a brief, stunned silence.

The Dalai Lama then answered. "The meaning of life is happiness."

He raised his finger, leaning forward, focusing on her as if she were the only person in the world. "Hard question is not, 'What is meaning of life?' That is easy question to answer! No, hard question is what make happiness. Money? Big house? Accomplishments? Friends? Or…"

He paused and answered the question like this: "Compassion and good heart."

That alone, he said, will bring happiness.

"Thank you," she said. "Thank you."

She got up and finished stacking the dirty dishes and cups and took them away.

I wonder what happened to that waitress. I wonder about the impact his words may have had on her life. Did the Dalai Lama inspire her to action? Was his answer the beginning of a new way of thinking for her? I hope so.

Summary

Only by adopting the HOPE worldview can one expect to make consistently good decisions, decisions that will lead to both satisfaction and contentment. How much better to be like the Dalai Lama and view the world through his HOPE perspective than the kind of worldview that led to the sad story of Joyce Vincent! In the next chapter, I will show the relationships between the FOPE, ROPE and MOPE worldviews and biases that may partially account for the situation in which Joyce found herself.

chapter 5

Biases (Thinking Anomalies) that Affect Decision-Making

Humans have always been fascinated by outer space. Since the beginning of time, we have been awed by the night sky, wondered about other galaxies, and dreamed of traveling beyond our planet. That's surely why so much science fiction has been written about space exploration and visiting other worlds.

For most of human history, though, space travel was just that—science fiction. But in this last century, humans have finally been able to get off the ground and into the air. It's pretty amazing that there were only 66 years between the Wright brothers taking their first flight in 1903 to humans landing on the moon in 1969.

However, since the moon landing, humans have not ventured any farther into the solar system. Voyager 1 in 2003 was the first man-made object to leave the solar system, but that was just a rocket ship sending back signals. No human was on board.

All that, however, might change. By the year 2025, if all goes according to plan, the Mars One project will establish a colony on Mars. In fact, the project leaders have been working to select a crew since 2013. By 2020, Mars One will plan to send material to Mars, and by 2024 the first crew will leave on a 210-day voyage for Mars. After that, a new crew will be sent every two years.

What an incredible venture! And according to the Mars One engineers, it can be done with present technology!

Who will be these new pioneers that will go to Mars? According to Mars One, more than 200,000 men and women from around the world responded to the first call for astronauts. Since then, the number of applicants has been whittled down to just over a thousand and in the end, only about 20 to 40 people will be selected for the project.

I can understand why some people might want to be part of such an exciting adventure. They would have the chance to explore new territory, step foot on new land much like Christopher Columbus and his crew.

However, I failed to mention one important point regarding the Mars One space adventure. The journey will be a one-way trip! All 200,000-plus applicants knew they would never return home to Planet Earth.

You see, Mars One has the technology to get astronauts to Mars, but it does not have the technology to get them back. When these crews leave for Mars, it will be permanent. They are not coming home.

And yet, despite the finality of the voyage—200,000 people chose to go?

How do you explain their decision-making process? What prompted them to apply for a one-way trip to Mars, knowing that they would never see their families or friends again? Why would a husband, a wife, a daughter, a brother choose to leave his/her family? Did they make rational decisions or emotional ones? What was it about the way they saw themselves, their existence, their world that motivated them to make such a life-changing choice?

Rival Decision-Making Models

The Mars One example serves as the crux of this book: how our worldview affects the kind of decisions we make. All of us, all the time, every day, make decisions, big and small, that reflect our worldview. And in turn, those decisions, good or bad, impact our lives.

I have argued that our worldviews—FOPE, ROPE, MOPE or HOPE—significantly impact the kind of decisions we make. I have also argued that to one degree or another, people fall into one of these groups, and it is from their orientation in one of these worldviews that they make their decisions. Finally, I have argued that the HOPE view, in contrast to the other three, is the best view to work from—the one worldview that has the best chance of positively impacting our decision-making.

In the past, decision-making was thought to be the result of rationally calculating the probability of a good outcome and then acting on that assessment. And that makes sense; it seems logical. In the process we would ask ourselves some of the following questions: What are the choices before me? What are the predicted outcomes of my choice? What choice has the highest probability of happiness?

What could be simpler or more rational than that?

However, Amos Tversky and Daniel Kahneman showed that we are not as rational as we once thought we were.[1] They proposed that our brains make quick judgments (decisions) by comparing what we are judging by some model in our mind. Unfortunately, these quick decisions allow the introduction of errors in our decision-making and limit our ability to make good decisions. We see all too often in our personal lives, as well as in those of others, how many of these decisions end up being anything but rational.

The husband who cheats with his administrative assistant at work, risking 30 years of marriage and two beautiful children.

The subcontractor who fires his best employee for fear of being passed over for a promotion.

The college student who hires a classmate to write his law-school application essay.

These decisions all seemed right at the moment they were made, but in the long-term, the choices were irrational.

Socrates once described man as a "rational animal." Maybe he should have described man as a being capable of rational thought but certainly not dominated by it.

And there's a reason for this, and it has to do with what I have been talking about in this book, our worldview. We make choices mostly based on how we view the world, and if we view the world in a skewed, distorted manner, there are bound to be flawed decisions especially when we are making quick ones.

I believe that three of the four worldviews are plagued with systematic weaknesses, which make them susceptible to certain thinking anomalies that cause flawed decisions, both big and small.

MOPE-Related Pitfalls

I first became aware of my own biases (thinking anomalies, as scientists are wont to call them) when my wife, Elissa, and I moved to Boston. We were fortunate to find a small, affordable, and charming light gray house that previously had been owned by two elderly women in a Boston suburb called Newton Hills. The inside of the house needed some remodeling, and we decided to paint the walls and purchase new curtains and carpeting. For curtains we chose a floral pattern in rust and gray that blended nicely with the house's exterior color. We also found a rust-colored carpet that complemented the curtains.

Elissa, however, was ambivalent about the shade of gray I chose for the walls. I felt confident because I had taken an art course at the San Francisco Art Institute during a summer in college and felt I had "an eye" for color. To demonstrate that I was right, I agreed to buy a pint of gray paint that I thought would match the carpet and curtains and apply it to a section of the wall. I was surprised when it didn't match. After a second failed attempt, I felt less confident and, eventually, left the color selection to Elissa and the man at the paint shop.

This might seem like a small incident; no one dies from poor interior decorating choices. But it speaks volumes about how reasonably intelligent and well-educated people can make wrong decisions, based on a false conception of themselves and the world in which they live.

In this example, I perceived myself to be smarter and more skilled than those around me, including the man at the paint shop. There's actually a name for this: *illusory superiority* in which your superiority is exactly that: an illusion. What might have caused me to be overconfident? Operating from a MOPE worldview caused me to think that my opinion was better than others. That was exactly my pitfall; I disregarded the opinion of my wife as well as that of the man at the paint shop who had more experience than I could acquire in my lifetime.

The idea that we are smarter, more skilled, and more attractive than others can actually be reinforced by selectively collecting data that supports our view. Have you ever asked a colleague how a certain color lipstick looks on you or asked your family about a new dish you just cooked for dinner? Rather than telling you the new color looks terrible or that the pasta is too bland—they endorse your actions. By not wanting to hurt your feelings, they inadvertently fall into the *confirmation bias* pitfall. The inaccurate or dishonest affirmation you get strengthens your perception that you are doing great.[2]

Besides the illusory superiority bias, there are a myriad of other ways, other means that have been identified as tools that we employ to compensate for or defend our egos. The table below provides a snapshot of some of the other specific "thinking anomalies" that I feel MOPE individuals are particularly susceptible to.

Table 4: Common MOPE-Related Pitfalls		
Name	**Definition**	**MOPE Response**
Self-supporting bias	Claiming more responsibility for successes than for failures	"That new marketing plan?—my idea."
Choice-supported bias	Remembering choices as better than they actually were	"That 27-hour road trip was a piece of cake."
False consensus bias	Assuming that those around us share our opinion	"It only makes sense to vote for my candidate: only an idiot wouldn't."
Fundamental attribution error	Inaccurately judging others without taking into account the context of the situation	"I can't believe that driver cut me off! What a jerk!" (as the driver speeds to the hospital with his pregnant wife).

Do any of these biases resonate with you? Do you find yourself falling into one of these traps or have you seen others close to you get stuck in these pitfalls? Again, these aren't issues that only MOPE individuals deal with; however, they do center on the need to support an elevated perception of self, which is most common in MOPEs.

ROPE-Related Pitfalls

Another group of thinking anomalies involves the fear of risks associated with uncertainty and/or the unknown, which is most commonly experienced by ROPEs. As we've already discussed, those with a ROPE worldview try to maintain a semblance of control possibly because of an underlying sense of insecurity. They thrive with specific rules, with set expectations and with order. Those of us with ROPE tendencies try to compensate for lack of control in a variety of ways. For example, when faced with uncertainty we may defer the decision or stick with the *status quo*.[3]

The aversion to uncertainty can also be partially attributed to *regret aversion*.[4] It has been shown that people experience about two times as much pain from a loss as compared to pleasure from a gain. This is the reason that economists give for investors buying bonds instead of stocks, since stocks are more volatile and risky even if they give much better returns. I've participated in research studies in which I've offered newer, better contrast materials (dyes) to patients having contrast CT studies of their brains. Many chose to be administered the older contrast, preferring a known risk to an unknown but probably smaller one associated with the new-and-improved contrast. When possible, some people want to reduce even a small risk to none (*zero-risk bias*), regardless of the cost.

Table 5 provides a snapshot of some of the specific "thinking anomalies" that I feel ROPE individuals are particularly prone to.

Because ROPEs have adopted a set of rules, a paradigm, a structure that makes them feel secure, they can be trapped in the status quo, trapped in the past.

How many businesses have faltered because their executives, happy about how things have worked in the past, failed to adjust to the future?

One classic story in the business world involves Firestone Tires. For many years it was at the top of its game, providing tires to the Detroit "Big Three" car-makers and others. For most of the twentieth century, the company did very well.

Table 5: Common ROPE-Related Pitfalls		
Name	**Definition**	**ROPE Response**
Ambiguity effect	Avoiding information that might make us feel uncertain	"We're choosing the fixed-rate mortgage: I don't care what my brother says about the rates possibly dropping during the next 10 years."
Illusion of control	Distorting reality to believe we can control it	"I'm not at all concerned about my daughter as a teenager. I know she'll always behave like we taught her to."
Prudence trap	Conservatively slanting one's judgment just to be safe	"I'm just making adjustments for the 'worst-case' scenario."
Just-world phenomenon	Believing people get what they deserve	"It was her fault. She shouldn't have dressed so provocatively."

Then in the 1970s everything changed. A French company, Michelin, introduced the radial tire to America. Based on a new design, the radial tires were all-around better tires—longer lasting, safer, and even more economical. Having already dominated the European market, the radials were soon on the path to dominating the American market.

The Firestone Company, however, remained caught up in its old ways. Yes, it started making radials, but following the rules and patterns of the past. It only tinkered with minor changes, never radically redoing their tires to meet the changing market. After all, the established patterns, the way things had always worked, had done the company well in the past. So why change?

Well, in the end, the company faltered, unable to compete.

Before long, it had lost much of its U.S. market to foreign corporations. It eventually went through two hostile takeover bids before Bridgestone, a Japanese company, bought it in 1988.

Clearly, ROPE worldviews can be held not just by individuals but also by large corporations.

FOPE-Related Pitfalls

German philosopher and writer Frederick Nietzsche expresses the FOPE worldview in his story "The Mad Man."[5]

> "Have you not heard of that madman who lit a lantern in the bright morning hours, ran to the market place, and cried incessantly: 'I seek God! I seek God!' As many of those who did not believe in God were standing around just then, he provoked much laughter. Has he gotten lost? asked one. Did he lose his way like a child? asked another. Or is he hiding? Is he afraid of us? Has he gone on a voyage? Emigrated? Thus, they yelled and laughed."

The hecklers that Nietzsche describes had abandoned their belief in God. For them, the whole idea of truth itself, with a capital T, was done. Gone. Truth for them was relative; truth is what works; truth is what you prefer. The same with morality. Human morality, like everything else, is man-made. It's like a preference for Gangsta Rap over Asian flute music or Expressionism over Egyptian tomb painting. There is no overarching narrative, no overarching story to guide us in right and wrong, or good and evil. Instead, we have to make up our own values along the way depending on how we feel. This epitomizes the FOPE post-modern worldview which has resulted in people who are more narcissistic and more anxious than ever.

The FOPE pitfalls are very real. It is difficult to live one's life without any unmovable guiding points. Table 6 provides a snapshot of some of the specific "thinking anomalies" that I feel FOPE individuals are particularly prone to.

Table 6: Common FOPE-Related Pitfalls		
Name	**Definition**	**ROPE Response**
Present value	Valuing immediate rewards more than long-term gains	"Let's go to the party; we can study later."
Positive outcome bias	Overestimating the probability of good things happening	"I'm sure things will work out!"
Attentional bias	Neglecting relevant information	"How was I supposed to know these pants weren't returnable?"
Recallability trap	Remembering dramatic events results in overestimating rare events	"I wouldn't fly on that airline: I remember they had a crash a couple of years ago."

Nature-Related Biases

The influences on decision-making I've been describing so far in this chapter I ascribe to nurture—the worldview we adopted, the ways we were raised, and the environment in which we grew up.

In contrast, I'll now briefly explore the influence that nature has on our decision-making, with nature being those forces and processes which we cannot control. For example, many experts in psychology feel that our personalities are genetically determined. Several systems exist for categorizing this basic aspect of our peersonalities, such as the Big Five personality dimensions or the Myers-Briggs classifications.[6, 7]

One school of thought regarding personality that has been around the longest divides personalities into four major types: choleric, sanguine, melancholy, and phlegmatic.[8] Cholerics are extroverts and tend to be strong-willed, productive and dynamic but who may sometimes have trouble getting along with others because they can be hot-headed, sarcastic, domineering, miserly and self-serving. Sanguines, also extroverts, tend to be outgoing, personable and carefree but can also be undependable, impulsive and fearful. There are two groups of introverts; one group includes the melancholics. They are gifted, perfectionistic, loyal, self-deprecating and thoughtful, but they are also prone to be suspicious, ultra-sensitive, moody and judgmental. Phlegmatics, the other group of introverts, are efficient, dependable and peaceful with happy temperaments but may lack emotion and motivation, and may also be cautious and indecisive.

People in each personality type appear to have a natural tendency to favor a particular worldview. If we placed the sanguines and melancholics along the chance-line, the sanguine would be at one end, roughly occupying the space dominated by the FOPE group. On the other end of the line would be melancholics, who, because of their perfectionistic tendencies, would likely occupy the space where the ROPEs reside. In between them in the contemplative zone would be indecisive phlegmatics with their aversion to conflict. The strong-willed cholerics, who are essentially self-serving, would be located away from the chance line and in the space occupied by MOPEs.

The natural tendency of a personality type to be attracted to one of these worldviews does not mean they will adopt it; people are free to choose and even change their worldview, as I will discuss in the next chapter.

Gender, another aspect of our nature, may also affect our decision-making. *Men Are From Mars, Women Are From Venus*, by John Gray, uses this planetary metaphor to describe the psychological differences he thinks exist between the sexes.[9] He contends that the genders react to stress differently and argues that when men's stress tolerance is exceeded, they tend to retreat and take "time outs." Women, on the other hand, like to talk about the situation with someone close.

Others have suggested that because women desire to form meaningful relationships, they will work hard to preserve them when they perceive there is a threat. Thus, when women are making decisions, they will consider how it will affect their network of family and friends. This characteristic has been attributed to women's larger prefrontal and anterior cingulate cortexes.[10] Men are said to be less interested in forming deep emotional relationships and thus more likely to have sex with strangers or even commit adultery. Some attribute these characteristics to the fact that men have larger amygdalae than women and thus are more prone to act with less restraint.

It should be noted that many academics are skeptical of these simplifications. In a *New York Times* article, Kate Taylor describes a continuing trend among college women who are replacing traditional dating practices by just "hooking up," a term that describes having a promiscuous sex life without committing to a relationship.[11] These college women now spend their time getting top grades and padding their resume with sports and community-service projects, as do their male counterparts, and focusing on getting leadership positions in student organizations and prestigious internships. These women assume that someone better will come along in their late 20s or early 30s when they are ready to commit. This mindset, previously attributed primarily to men, may demonstrate that changing social values are as influential as gender differences or it may be that they are just changing from a HOPE or ROPE to a MOPE worldview.

Other thinking anomalies that may be nature-related because of their universality are those related to time. The human tendency to weigh recent events more heavily than earlier ones is called the *recency effect*. The tendency to remember past events more positively than they actually were is called the *rosy retrospective*. .

A whole slew of quirks are related to our inability to properly weigh and assess different factors and information items. For instance, we tend to give disproportionately greater weight to initial information, paying less attention to things we learn later. Another quirk is overlooking the frequency of an occurrence when making a decision (*base-rate trap*). An example presented in *Smart Choices* asks us to decide what is more likely: is a quiet, sedate male more apt to be a librarian or a salesman?[12] Almost everyone guesses librarian. However, they fail to take into account that salesmen outnumber male librarians 100:1; thus, even if quiet, sedate salesmen are rare, they are more prevalent than quiet, sedate male librarians. Closely related to this bias is our tendency to incorrectly assume that specific conditions are more probable than general ones (*conjunction fallacy*) or to judge the whole to be less than its parts (*sub-additivity effect*). We may also overlook the fact that extreme conditions are rare (*regression to the mean*).

The brain has a disturbing method of dealing with complex situations. Imagine an experiment in which the participants are presented with two choices. When the results are counted, each option gets roughly 50 percent of the votes. If a third choice is added, one would expect the third choice to steal votes equally from both of the first two. Instead, preference for one of the original two choices increases dramatically. In one experiment a choice that initially received 53 percent increased to 72 percent when one more option was added.[13] In another study, California grocery shoppers were offered either six different kinds of jams on a display table or 24 kinds at a separate time. The group that was offered 24 choices bought no jam.[14] In contrast, the group that was offered six jams actually bought jams. This research may support the claim that our minds can handle only up to seven pieces of data at a time.

Finally, we can also be influenced by subtle changes in how information is presented (*framing trap*). I enjoyed watching the effect of the framing trap on one of my favorite TV shows—*Pawn Stars*. People come to the shop to pawn or sell a variety of their valuables. The pawn shop owner studies the object and then offers a price, thus framing the range of the negotiation. If the customer objects that the offered price is too low, the pawnbroker may raise his offer slightly, but within the bounds of the initial frame, saying that he will have difficulty in either disposing of the object or that he has to make a profit to stay in business. In fact, most retail stores that sell clothes frame what they claim is a reasonable price by setting it as high as the competition will allow early in the season in order to maximize profits, only to lower it later at the end of the season.

Can Nature-Related Biases be Changed?

Politicians, social scientists, educators and many others strive to improve our environment since they think they can change us (nurture) for the better. In contrast, almost no one tries to change our nature because most informed people think it's impossible (Chapter 2). However, I presented a case study to show that it is possible to change nature. In Chapter 4, I refer to a HOPE quote made by a choleric, the apostle Paul, in which he encourages us to humbly look out for the interests of others. Earlier in his life he was a rabid Jewish ROPE who not only followed the rules but vigorously persecuted those who didn't. When he caught early Jewish Christians breaking Jewish laws, he imprisoned them and on at least one occasion even executed one of them. If Paul could change, anyone can change! In fact, later in life he even defined the HOPE worldview to the Corinthian Christians as being patient, kind and willing to pursue truth. Furthermore, it is not jealous, proud or irritable.[15]

In the story of the father and his two sons in Chapter 1, the younger son who had a FOPE worldview and a sanguine personality appears to have arrived at a more realistic view of his father and the farm by the end of the story. However, the story does not tell us if he evolved to a HOPE worldview. I certainly hope he did.

Tim LaHaye tells us how the weaknesses associated with the major personality types can be made into strengths and thus help us improve our interpersonal relationships with others if we are willing to change to a HOPE worldview.[8] Similarly, some of the other negative nurture factors described in the previous sections can become strengths if we adopt the HOPE worldview.

Completing the Decision-Making Diagram by Incorporating Biases

The biases/thinking anomalies described in this chapter are related to either the perception we have of ourselves and those around us or the values and preferences that result from them because of our worldview or a poorly functioning feedback loop. As a result of the thinking anomalies described in this chapter, I have added biases/thinking anomalies to the solution box in Fig.12. However, it's probable that some of the genetically-based biases should be placed to the left of worldview.

Adding biases/thinking anomalies to the thinking flowchart that was introduced in Chapter 1 completes that diagram. The solution box is again placed to the right of worldview in order to illustrate that worldview dominates our thinking. Again, many of the biases described in this chapter are the result of our quick, flawed estimates of perceived good outcomes. By choosing the wrong worldview, we subject ourselves to a number of pitfalls that will only perpetuate a sub-optimal decision-making process.

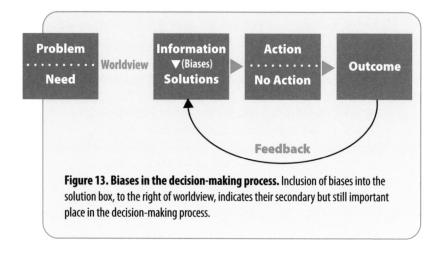

Figure 13. Biases in the decision-making process. Inclusion of biases into the solution box, to the right of worldview, indicates their secondary but still important place in the decision-making process.

Summary

I believe that many of the biases/thinking anomalies described in this chapter are related to specific worldviews. Individuals who adopt the ROPE and FOPE worldviews need to feel good about themselves by either creating a world of certainty in order to be happy or experience "highs" in order to feel alive. For the ROPE group, it may mean associating with a church that claims to have the ultimate truth or an organization that has a unique environmental or humanitarian goal. For the FOPE group, it may mean finding ways to stimulate themselves so they feel alive. For the MOPEs it means creating a reality in which they perceive themselves as smarter, more skilled, and more attractive than their peers. Regardless, I believe many of these thinking anomalies can be gradually corrected or attenuated by adopting the HOPE worldview. When we have an accurate picture of ourselves and when we don't have to fight so hard to defend our self-esteem, we are less susceptible to these pitfalls! By focusing on others, on opportunities to help those around us thrive, our purpose in life will become clearer and we will have greater life satisfaction.

Author David Foster Wallace in his now-famous Kenyon College graduation address said this about dealing with frustrating people:

> But most days, if you're aware enough to give yourself a choice, you can choose to look differently at this fat, dead-eyed, over-made-up lady who just screamed at her kid in the checkout line. Maybe she's not usually like this. Maybe she's been up three straight nights holding the hand of a husband who is dying of bone cancer. Or maybe this lady is the low-wage clerk at the motor vehicle department, who just yesterday helped your spouse resolve a horrific, infuriating, red-tape problem through some small act of bureaucratic kindness.[16]

How to change to a better worldview will be discussed in the next chapter.

chapter 6

How to Change to a Better Worldview

The famous Holocaust survivor and Nazi-hunter, Simon Wiesenthal, told a harrowing story of his escape from death.[1] During a roundup of Jews in the Ukraine in 1941, he said that he had been part of a group of Jews lined up facing a wall by Ukrainian auxiliary troops, whom the Nazis often used to do their killings. The troops, swigging Vodka, started shooting people in the back of their necks. Bodies fell and fell. As he heard the executioners getting closer to him, he stared blankly into the wall. Then suddenly he heard church bells ringing. Instantly, the shooting stopped, and a Ukrainian shouted, "Enough! Time for evening mass!" The men left, and Wiesenthal escaped.

An incredible story, on numerous levels. But with regard to worldviews and how they impact our decision-making, this one is quite instructive. Who were these men that could take their own neighbors, line them up, and then shoot them? This didn't happen in a moral vacuum. This example, and the Holocaust in general, is an example of the MOPE/ROPE worldview—they were simply doing what they were ordered to do, first by their Nazi master and then, second, when the bells rang, by their church!

As we have seen all along, our worldview greatly impacts the kinds of decisions we make. Thus, the question becomes, if we have a wrong worldview, one that leads us to make bad decisions, how do we change to a better worldview? I trust by now you are convinced it's the HOPE worldview.

Maybe you're shaking your head and saying, "I can't see my way through this. I've been looking out for myself for so long that I simply don't know how to do otherwise."

Barriers to Change

There are certainly significant reasons that make people feel they can't change. For starters, many people are reluctant to face uncertainty. Those in the ROPE group like the status quo because it makes them feel in control and gives them a sense of worth and security. They cling to their rules, their standards and their expectations because it makes them feel reasonably comfortable. Although they may be somewhat bored and discontented with life, they don't see any really compelling reasons to change. Although the MOPE group may not be as concerned with uncertainty, they also may not want to change—but for different reasons. What if they lose their power, their wealth and their status? Looking out for themselves has gotten them pretty far; it's hard for them to imagine how putting others first would yield the same or better results. The FOPEs look at the lifestyles of the ROPEs and HOPEs and find them so boring that they aren't tempted to try it!

Another barrier to change may be the individuals with whom we associate in each of these groups. An article in the *Harvard Business Review* recounts a study that examined the positive and negative impact of those around us:

> In one study, we asked a group of college students to solve 20 math problems in a very short time. No one could realistically solve all the problems within the allotted time. We told participants that we would pay them for whatever problems they reported they had solved. The money they could earn was placed in an envelope on their desks. After the allotted time was up, students were supposed to check their own performance, pay themselves, shred the test, and leave. The math task, however, was just a pretense for the real experiment, which concerned cheating.[2]

Not long after the test started, one of the students claimed that he had finished all the problems. Everyone else in the room knew that was impossible. Yet, the student (who was really a paid actor) took all the cash that was available to him and walked out. Thus, the other students, taking the test, just assumed that he had cheated.

What effect did that have on them? It showed that the overall cheating of other students increased when they believed that someone else had cheated.

My conclusion: The morals of those around us can be contagious if we live on or below the chance line.

Yes, the influence of close associates around us does matter. They can have a significant effect on our ability to change or not change our worldview.

Change Is Possible Because of Neuroplasticity

The world we live in constantly inundates us with everything but the HOPE worldview. The focus of most social media can be overwhelmingly self-centered, encouraging FOPE and MOPE individuals everywhere to keep putting up selfies, keep boasting about their perfect lives, keep vying for the most likes or re-tweets. In our professional lives we are taught to compete with others rather than reach out to help our colleagues. Instead, we cross our arms and wait for them to fail, capitalizing on their shortcomings to our advantage. ROPE and MOPE thinkers do succeed socially and professionally but frequently to the detriment of their relationships with others.

It's hard to swim against the current, to counter the messages we are surrounded by and to choose an alternate path.

But you can! As a neuroscientist, I can say with great confidence that your brain is *built for change.* "Your experience with the world alters your brain's structure, chemistry, and genetic expression, often profoundly, throughout your life," write Steven Quartz and Terrence Sejnowski.[3] Dendrites can be pruned when an area of the brain is underutilized or they can be expanded when the need arises. When a small area of the brain is destroyed, as in a small stroke, the brain is capable of creating new pathways around the injured area to regain the lost function, or sometimes it may actually create a new center. This is called *neuroplasticity*: it's the ability of the brain to physically and functionally reorganize itself![4, 5]

So, if you change your worldview, you can change your brain, and in the process change how you make decisions. The catalyst for change may be a crisis when one's core assumptions are shown to be wrong. A religious ROPE person who believes he is protected if he prays for safety before taking a driving trip will experience a crisis when his car is hit by a drunk driver and his wife and children are critically injured. He is justified in asking himself whether God agreed to be his bodyguard. In the end, one can hope that this self-examination will lead him to a more realistic view of the relationship that God has with him.

The time it takes to change worldviews may be quick, but more likely it will take years. Nicole Antoinette, in her blog, states that people frequently ask her for the secret of how she motivated herself to get into shape.[6] She states: "It took me 26 years of unused gym memberships, unopened workout DVDs, and half-completed body boot camp challenges to finally develop a regular exercise routine. Twenty-six [an expletive] years."

Those with a ROPE worldview may find it the hardest to change. Jonathan Haidt, author of *Righteous Mind*, states: "Moral attributes are especially difficult to change" because emotions are attached to these preferences.[7] This is because those with the ROPE view are often convinced that they are doing the right thing, the moral thing, the thing that (in some cases) they believe that God wants them to do. Especially in the latter case, it becomes very hard to change.

The fact that changing worldviews is more difficult the older one gets may be an incentive to address this issue as early in life as possible. It may also be an important reason for parents to create a HOPE environment while their children are still developing their worldviews.

How I Changed

Some authors suggest that recognition of one's problem leads to a new way of solving problems, which in conjunction with a firm commitment (willpower), leads to change. This process has been called the transtheoretical model and consists of five states: pre-contemplation, contemplation, preparation, action, and maintenance.[8]

In the pre-contemplative stage one questions or even becomes disillusioned with one's current method of making decisions. In the contemplative stage one considers new strategies to stop making the same mistakes. I'm uncertain which one of these two stages is more important but both are necessary either consciously or unconsciously before change can occur.

I suspect that I was in the pre-contemplative stage when I began observing my wife's capacity to have more meaningful relationships with both her students and colleagues than I was having. In other words, my feedback loop was telling me that the outcomes I desired weren't there. It was precisely at this time that I was listening to recorded studies by a theologian named Graham Maxwell, Ph.D. He summarized his ideas in a book called *Servants or Friends*; his description of servants paralleled my ROPE group, and his friends paralleled my HOPE group.[9] Once I realized that I had a MOPE/HOPE mentality that was limiting my relationships with others, I began contemplating the HOPE worldview.

My transition to a HOPE worldview was further facilitated by the role model I have previously mentioned, Dr. Jack Thornbury. Before Dr. Thornbury arrived in the Radiology Department of the University of Rochester, New York, I viewed him as a competitor because I knew he was to be appointed chief of the body CT section. I assumed he would be able to demonstrate the usefulness of CT to the clinical departments he would be serving, and thus reduce the time I had on the same scanner to support the neurologists, neurosurgeons, and orthopedic surgeons who worked in the hospital. I was concerned because I was already having difficulty keeping up with their urgent demands. I might have been even more concerned if I had known that Dr. Thornbury was a recognized world authority in body imaging.

Within a year of Dr. Thornbury's arrival, I was also appointed director of the newly formed Magnetic Resonance Imaging section and became aware that a part of my job would be to help New York State determine the usefulness of this new technology. When I told my department chairman that I wasn't sure of the best way of doing this evaluation, he suggested I speak to Dr. Thornbury. My chairman told me that Dr. Thornbury was a national authority in designing clinical scientific studies and that I might benefit from his expertise. I swallowed my pride and approached him late one afternoon in his office. Though surrounded by stacks of patient files and films, he put everything aside and gave me his undivided attention and helped me design a very good study. He showed me how to fill the boxes in a 2 x 2 table with data that I would lbe collecting that would satisfy the state's demand to evaluate this new technology. More important, he helped me to transition into the HOPE worldview. He provided me with a role model who lived and breathed the HOPE worldview. So how did Dr. Thornbury help me transition to the HOPE worldview? It occurred, in part, through specialized neurons in my brain called mirror neurons.

Mirror Neurons Aid Change

Although no one is certain exactly how mirror neurons work, some investigators have speculated that one of their functions is to mirror what they see.[10, 11] We can observe this, especially with small children, who constantly mirror what they see. Artists, writers, singers—they all often find someone whom they admire and whom they seek to emulate, to mirror, to learn from. Who hasn't experienced, either in a good way or a bad way, how observation and contact influence our own behavior?

In my case, these neurons helped me to transition to the HOPE worldview by just being around Dr. Thornbury. The expression, "A man is known by the company he keeps," tells only part of the story. The other part is that we also become like the company we keep; if they have good traits like those that Dr. Thornbury had, we can acquire them.[12, 13] As I said earlier, all this happened to me unconsciously because my mirror neurons were busy copying Dr. Thornbury's good traits. A business consultant observed:

> "... employees ... were virtually failing at their jobs because they could not focus on getting work done. They were always gossiping or sending chain emails because that is what their friends at work did. After waking up to the fact that maybe their friends were causing their performance problems, they distanced themselves from those friends, and it was like they were a new person: They became among the best employees in the organization."[14]

The concept that we influence our friends and acquaintances that make up our network has been documented by Nicholas

Christakes and James Fowler, who observed that happiness can spread out in our network: those who are close friends or in the immediate family experience the largest benefit, while those who are somewhat removed receive lesser benefit.[15] Unhappiness can also spread through the network, but the effect is less. Norman Corwin has explored this concept.

> "But good can be as communicable as evil, and that is where kindness and compassion come into play. So long as conscionable and caring people are around, so long as they are not muted or exiled, so long as they remain alert in thought and action, there is a chance for contagions of the right stuff . . . ."[13]

Elsewhere, he says:

> "The blood relatives of common courtesy are kindness, sympathy and consideration. And the reward for exercising them is to feel good about having done so. When a motorist at an intersection signals to another who's waiting to join the flow of traffic, "Go ahead, it's OK. Move in," and the recipient of the favor smiles and makes a gesture of appreciation, the giver enjoys a glow of pleasure. It's a very little thing, but it represents something quite big."[13]

Friends (Hierarchical Versus Participatory Relationships)

If my hypothesis that changing to a HOPE worldview can be facilitated by having friends with a HOPE worldview is correct, it is important to understand something about friendship. Research suggests that the basis for friendship is related to three major factors: proximity; repeated, unplanned interactions; and settings where individuals can engage in intimate, confidential conversations.

Alex Williams, in his *New York Times* article, contends that making close friends is a function of age.[16] High schools, colleges, and universities are the ideal environment for making friends because students are forced into sustained contact with one another during which time they develop common experiences, both good and bad, that they can talk about. Not surprisingly, most people state that they had the most friends during this phase of their lives. Later, when they transition into the workplace, they find it much harder to make close friends. Workplace friends can be problematic: there is competition for promotion and pay; there is suspicion that others may like you for secondary gains; and, finally, it is difficult to develop meaningful friendships when you know that your acquaintance may be transferred or is planning to quit in the near future. These considerations become amplified as one transitions into middle age, when one becomes even more selective about friends. If one enters a permanent relationship, it will be necessary to satisfy one's partner's taste in friends, and, if one has children, it will also be necessary to make sure that the children like each other. Thus, it is not surprising that more and more people are making Facebook friends. An explosion in the pet population in Western countries has also occurred during the past 40 years. One researcher says, "What's happening is simply that we're allowing animals to fill the gap in our lives."[17] We are purchasing friends.

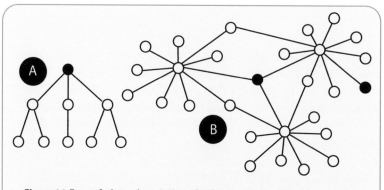

Figure 14. Types of relationships. A: Hierarchical command. The dark circle represents the leader. The open circles represent all the people who follow the leader. B: Participatory network. The open circles represent all the individuals who are actively engaged in the network. The dark circles represent individuals who do not contribute to the network.
Adapted from an illustration by Danilo Boskovic

In contrast to the FOPE, ROPE, and MOPE friends that Alex Williams describes, are friendships that HOPE people can offer. As I stated earlier, my change in worldview was facilitated through my wife and Dr. Thornbury, who both had HOPE worldviews. The interactions one can have with HOPE-minded individuals are analogous to being a part of a participatory network[18] (Figure 13-B).

In the participatory network, individuals are important because of their willingness to share either their experience or the information they possess. The freedom that individuals feel when utilizing the network allows them to share their ideas and insights, ask questions, and even receive answers and thus learn, grow and create. Although some individuals may be more important than others, everyone has value since everyone's experience and skills are different. If a person does not contribute to the network, he/she will be eventually discovered and either bypassed or isolated.

In contrast, in a hierarchical structure people are expected to give deference to those with prestige or influence (Figure 13-A). Stability in the hierarchical system is based on either rewards or fear. Learning is not a major concern of this system—obedience and conformity are. Friendships in this system are based on whether there are benefits from the relationship.

The participatory type of system is more stable than the hierarchical system because, rather than being dependent on just one person, the network draws strength from many sources. Similarly, participatory relationships are more stable since they allow individuals with common intersts to pursue common objectives and develop meaninful relationships. Hierarchical relationships are less stable and usually end when external constraints are gone.

Characteristics of HOPE Friends

If you want to adopt a HOPE worldview surround yourself with HOPE people. But what character traits can you expect to find in individuals with a HOPE worldview with whom you can begin to form a healthy participatory network? You can get some clues from reviewing excerpts from a letter written by Arial Kaminer, a *New York Times* editor, to her friend David Rakoff, who was dying of cancer:[19]

David,

. . . I've never told you how much I've learned from you. Here is the simplest lesson you taught me: Don't trade up. Don't grade friendships on a hierarchical scale . . . . Don't value people based on some external indicator of status. Don't take a competitive view of your social life . . . . I truly can't tell you how many seemingly complicated situations it resolved into clarity and fairness. I am grateful to you for that.

Here is another: As fun as it might seem to be drunk and witty and cutting, it's probably better in the long run to be kind . . . . It seems insane, or worse, that I didn't have that epiphany until I was 40—years after I had aged out of those drunk-witty-and-cutting nights out on the town . . . . But until I read your essay, I had not put away childish things. You grew me up.

Here is a third. It's the big one: Be grateful and humble and mean it . . . . Humility should be easier for me than for you to practice. I don't have millions of people racing to their radios to listen to me, devouring my books, guffawing at my jokes, applauding my performances, crying at my movies. And gratitude should be easier for me, too, because for God's sake, I don't have metastatic cancer. But it isn't. I still lose sight of the big picture and feel petulant and entitled. Thinking about you helps.

. . . Your friendship is a powerful force. You bake bread, paint denim jackets, craft pear lanterns, adapt screenplays, pay sickbed visits, slice freezer cookies and give home décor consults for more people than I'll ever meet. I can't do what you do, but I think about what motivates your kindness, and I try to learn from that. I've done it from the earliest days of our friendship, and I plan to keep at it for a great many years to come.

Thank you for giving me that chance, and for being my friend.

Love, Arial

Arial's letter describes two traits—humility and gratitude—that her friend David possessed and that we should look for in a friend if we want to change to a HOPE worldview. David's humility, I believe, gave him the freedom to embrace others because he didn't have to be critical of them to inflate his self-esteem.[20] Furthermore, he could unreservedly praise others when they did something exceptional because he was free of envy and jealousy. David's type of humility did not make him a cringing, self-effacing coward who thought it virtuous to be forgotten, undervalued, and taken for granted. Instead, people wanted to be around him because he was both funny and creative and, most of all, because he was a caring person who enjoyed helping people achieve their potential.

The other important trait that Arial admired in David was gratitude.[21] Those who possess this trait acknowledge kind acts that others have performed in contrast to those who feel entitled to such acts. Gratitude leads to a more generous spirit of giving without thinking about secondary gains. Grateful people are also likable because they tend to be optimistic and hopeful.[22] A benefit of having a grateful, optimistic spirit is that it can result in a healthier, happier, and longer life.[23] Although the exact relationship between happiness and health is controversial, there is some evidence to suggest that happiness has a positive effect on the immune system.[24]

What HOPE Friendships are All About

Good friendships that are deep and long-lasting happen because each friend puts the other friend's best interest first. Each practices a HOPE worldview when it comes to the other person.

Let me give you an example of a HOPE friendship. Thomas Hudner grew up in a privileged home in Fall River, Massachusetts.[25] Not exactly the Kennedys but well enough off, even during the Depression. In 1939, as a young man, Hudner entered the prestigious Phillips Academy in Andover, Massachusetts. His family had a long history in the Academy, which his father and uncle attended.

Following the attack on Pearl Harbor and the United States' entry into the War with Japan, Hudner heard a speech by the Academy headmaster that inspired him to join the military. In 1943, he had preregistered at Harvard University. His father was a Harvard man, and everyone expected Tom to follow in his footsteps.

But to everyone's surprise, Tom contacted his congressman and secured a nomination to the Naval Academy. He was accepted and graduated in May 1946, nine months after World War II ended. Three years later in 1949 he received his Wings of Gold and was assigned to Fighter Squadron 32 aboard the USS Leyte. Thomas Hudner was a navy pilot about the time the United States entered the Korean War.

The next part of this story takes place two years before Tom Hudner was born. In the Deep South, in Hattiesburg, Mississippi, another boy was born. Although Hattiesburg was only about 1,200 miles from Fall River, Massachusetts, it might have been on a different continent. You see, Jesse Brown was born to a black sharecropper family.

Young Jesse experienced first-hand the racism that blacks experienced at that time in the South. Yet, as a child, he developed an interest in flying and hoped to be a pilot. One day, while watching a plane fly by as he worked in the fields, he told the other farmhands that he wanted to fly. They laughed at him and said, "If they don't let us blacks ride in planes, what makes you think you can be flying one?"

In July 1946 he enlisted in the U.S. Naval Reserve; in April 1947 he accepted an appointment as a midshipman in the U.S. Navy; and in 1948, amid a lot of press coverage, he earned his pilot wings.

A black Navy officer was rare enough in America at that time. But Jesse L. Brown was the first African-American aviator in the U.S. Navy. That was big news. He even made LIFE magazine.

In January 1949, Jesse L. Brown was assigned to Fighter Squadron 32 aboard the USS Leyte, the same squadron and ship as Tom Hudner. He, too, had become a Navy pilot as the United States was entering the Korean War.

And in this context, Hudner's and Brown's paths crossed. Both were navy pilots in the Korean War, both in Fighter Squadron 32. Despite their different backgrounds, they grew to deeply respect each other and became friends.

Our story takes place during the battle of the Chosin Reservoir on a frigid December day in 1950. When it seemed that the war was being won by the Allies, hundreds of thousands of Chinese troops suddenly poured into Korea, and the ground game changed dramatically. About 8,000 Marines and Army Infantry soldiers were trapped in the Chosin Reservoir as an overwhelming force of Chinese soldiers moved in on them. The Americans were fighting for their very lives.

Here's where the Navy pilots, including Hudner and Brown, came in. In their F4U Corsairs, on December 4, 1950, they were doing all they could to protect the troops below by bombing, strafing, and even dropping napalm on advancing Chinese troops.

The Chinese didn't take kindly to having their troops burned alive with napalm. In other words, you couldn't drop napalm on people and expect any downed pilot not to be tortured or killed if caught. Rumor had it that helicopter pilots at Chosin were now dressing like ground Marines so that if they were shot down they could deny that they were pilots.

Whatever the risks, these pilots were doing their jobs, and things seemed to be going well. Then Hudner noticed that Brown's plane was spewing oil. An enemy bullet had punctured his plane's oil line. Quickly, the plane's 18 pistons were melting inside the engine.

They all knew what was going to happen. Brown was going to crash in enemy territory—and that's exactly what happened.

At first, the others flying above all assumed that Jesse L. Brown, the U.S. Navy's first black pilot, had died. But as they circled overhead, they could see that Jesse had pulled the canopy back. He was alive! But he wasn't making radio contact.

Even worse, they saw smoke starting to pour out of his engine which would give away his location to the Chinese. Yet Brown wasn't moving. At that point they realized that either he was trapped in the plane, or too injured to move, or both. Either way, they knew that unless something drastic happened, Brown was dead.

Hudner knew the rules. A downed pilot was to be left alone by other pilots. The skipper had told them that rule, explicitly, and that any man who broke it would be court-martialed. But even though they had called for a rescue helicopter, it might not get there in time.

"I'm going in," Hudner radioed the other pilots. They were dead silent. Either they didn't understand what he meant, or they didn't want to encourage him on what could be a suicide mission.

Then, against all rules, Hudner crash landed his plane into the snow near Jesse's downed plane. That crash alone could have killed him, but it didn't. He jumped out of his wrecked plane and ran over to Jesse.

Hudner told Jesse that he was there to rescue him. And Brown was so grateful! But he was also severely injured and, worse, trapped in the plane. Hudner couldn't get him out. By throwing snow on the burning engine Hudner was at least able to contain the fire that threatened to burn Brown alive. Their only hope was the rescue helicopter getting there before the Chinese did. If not, they would be taken as POWs and most likely starved to death, the Chinese way of making a political statement.

Finally, the rescue helicopter came. They worked and worked but still couldn't get him out. They would need a torch, which they didn't have. Then, to their dismay, Brown died right there, still trapped in the cockpit of his downed plane.

Now, Hudner was left with a different choice. Stay there with the body and wait for the rescue team to come back with a torch, or leave Brown's body there and get out. If the rescue plane didn't get back in time, he'd either freeze to death or be captured by the Chinese. Hating to do it, he left. All the risks that he took, the danger that he faced—in the end, some would say it was all for nothing. His pilot friend, the one he risked everything to save, had died.

Though Hudner broke the rules, he later received the Medal of Honor for his actions, for demonstrating what friendship is all about.

Sure, we're not all going to become Thomas Hudner, and certainly not overnight. But our brains have been built for change, and we can move in the direction of a HOPE worldview if we can find HOPE friends or HOPE mentors.

HOPE Mentoring

In his book *Coach*, Michael Lewis reminisces of his high school baseball coach, Bill Fitzgerald—a man who knew how to help his players reach their potential, not only as baseball players but as human beings.[26] Lewis attended a Jewish-oriented New Orleans preparatory high school for the wealthy, where he began to play for coach Fitzgerald. A year after Lewis began playing, Fitz entered their team into a better league. His team began losing and in the process became increasingly listless and indifferent. However, change occurred after a game when a base runner failed to slide when he was instructed to by Fitz. The coach held a post-game workout, where he had his players run and slide until their uniforms were dirty and in some cases torn and bloody. At the end of the session, Fitz declared that they were not to wash their uniforms until they won their first game.

Fitz's team wore their foul, dirty uniforms to their next game. Opposing teams were initially amused but became increasing alarmed and then, just plain scared by a team that took playing baseball so seriously. After each loss, Fitz told them "what it means to be a man."[27]

A man, he said, would struggle against his natural instincts to run from adversity. He also taught them how to fight against fear and failure.

His high expectations and relentless honesty in dealing with his players helped them develop the discipline that transformed them from spoiled, privileged, egocentric kids to true teammates and later into successful adults. Fitz was a real mentor to his players by practicing tough love—a combination of discipline and altruism that worked because his players learned to trust him. Lewis said:

> "We listened to the man because he had something to tell us, and us alone. Not how to play baseball, though he did that better than anyone. Not how to win, though winning was wonderful. Not even how to sacrifice. He was teaching us something far more important: how to cope with the two greatest enemies of a well-lived life, fear and failure."[28]

> "And finally, somehow, we won. No one who walked into our locker room as we danced around and hurled our uniforms into the washing machine,

and listened to the speech Fitz gave about our fighting spirit, would have known they were looking at a team that stood 1-12."[28]

Coach Fitz let his team experience the difference between short-lived feelings of pleasure and long-term satisfaction that comes from being virtuous. That is why Fitz emphasized "becoming a man." Later in life, this would mean his players would be involved in activities that would make the world a better place in which to live.

Determining a person's passion (purpose) in life is a good way to find out whether he or she has a HOPE worldview that promotes growth. Fitz's passion to change spoiled, affluent, privileged kids into men who were willing to face "fear and failure" resulted in long-lasting relationships that motivated his players to support him both emotionally and financially later in their lives.

Barriers to HOPE Mentoring

Years later, while some of Fitz's former players were raising money to redo the gym and name it after him because of how he had changed their lives, other parents were trying to get Fitz fired because they felt he was too hard on their kids. So, Lewis came back to New Orleans to see what was happening. Fitz told him that he had to adapt. "I've had to learn that you can't save everybody," he said. "I mean some of them will never understand the responsibility they have to their team and themselves."[29] Lewis understood what Fitz was talking about. He recalled an incident that occurred many years before when he chose to go skiing during the Mardi Gras break instead of staying behind to practice with the team. Soon after the break he was asked to pitch and began throwing balls. After each bad pitch he heard Fitz in the dugout ask, "Where was Michael Lewis during Mardi Gras?" Lewis became acutely aware that Fitz was pointing out his disregard for the well-being of the team. Lewis never made that mistake again.

Summary

The underlying premise of this book has been the undeniable need for a HOPE worldview. We've seen this worldview expressed by the father through his relationship with his two sons, by Jack Thornbury, Tom Hudner, Nelson Mandela and Bill Fitzgerald. I have also shown you the flip side of that: the three worldviews that can be self-serving and destructive. The contrast in these four worldviews is stark and the consequences are indeed very real. One leads to a life filled with meaning and value, a life that brings about contentment and true happiness, while the others produce short-lived pleasures and missed opportunities.

We all have the ability to choose the HOPE worldview. By first recognizing our current mindset and choosing to reframe it in a different context, we can imagine what we'd really like to be. We can then make intentional choices to surround ourselves with people who already possess those traits and are willing to help us achieve our goals. We may need to distance ourselves from some individuals while being purposeful about connecting with others.

And, finally, we simply need to *try*. Change is never easy, especially when it involves changing something as significant and foundational as our worldview. It can be a difficult and perhaps a long process to break old habits, habits that always put ourselves first or lead us to judge others, but it can be done. Change is possible. Remember, *our brains are built for change.*

Rabbi Abraham Twerski, M.D., founder and medical director of Gateway Rehabilitation Center, tells of a speaking visit to Tel Aviv, Israel, where he was visiting a sister rehabilitation center. While he was speaking about self-esteem, Avi, a disheveled, hunched-over man asked, "How can you talk to us of this? I've been in and out of jail for half of my 34 years. I've been a thief since I was eight. When I'm out of prison, I can't find work and my family doesn't want to see me."[30]

Rabbi Twerski stopped him and asked him if he had passed a jewelry store lately. "The diamond you saw in the window was once a dirty lump of rock, but someone saw its intrinsic beauty and was able to bring it out." Twerski went on to say, "You're like that dirt-covered ore, and our business is to find the diamond within and polish it until it glows."

Two years passed. Then one day, the manager of the rehabilitation center needed help and asked Avi to carry a couch someone had donated to the center. Avi agreed, and while carrying the couch into the center, an envelope fell out. In the envelope Avi found five thousand shekels (about $1,700). What was a man who had been a thief since age eight to do?

Avi chose to tell the manager, who, in turn, reported it to the donor. The donor was so gratified that the family said the center could keep the money. When Avi relayed this story to Rabbi Twerski, he wrote, "When I used drugs, I would get a high for a very short time; and when it wore off, I felt terrible, worse than before. It's been three months since I found that money, and every time I think of what I did, I feel good all over again." Maybe Avi felt good because he knew he had done the right thing and more important, that he was no longer a thief!

There is more to life than regrets, poor choices and disappointing outcomes. With the knowledge you now possess, you can move away from your present reality and from the artifice of self-serving, rule-clinging satisfaction. The good news is that although not easy you can change your worldview; you can experience that long-lasting feeling of contentment, that genuine joy that comes from putting others first, that comes from choosing the HOPE worldview as Avi did.

epilogue

If you are uncertain about your worldview, there is a Worldview Inventory (WIN) that can help you determine your worldview. This instrument has been shown to reliably identify worldviews among adults and middle and high schoolers. The WIN which consists of around 50 questions comes in two versions: Adult (18 years and older) and Student (12-17 years). It takes approximately 15 minutes to complete and can be taken either online or on paper.

Make Your Choices Better Than Chance contends that your happiness and well-being is related to your worldview which, in turn, impacts your decision-making. Preliminary research using the WIN and standardized student achievement and ability tests indicates that there may also be a relationship between worldview and academic achievement. In one four-year longitudinal study and a cohort of over 50,000 students, the unexpected finding that students increased in both achievement and ability has led to much discussion about the factors that might be responsible—particularly for the increase in ability. Some researchers hypothesize that worldview may be one of those factors and are currently investigating this idea.

For more information about the Worldview Inventory and how you may take it or utilize it in your research, contact the Center for Research on Adventist k-12 Education (CRAE) at La Sierra University: crae@lasierra.edu or 951.785.2997.

references

chapter 1

1. Stockton, F. *The Lady or the Tiger*. New York: Charles Scribner' Sons, 1884.

2. Iyengar, S. Columbia University study: *The Art of Choosing*. 2010.

3. This story is adapted from Luke 15: 11-32. New International Version, 1987.

4. Smith, H.W. *What Matters Most*. New York: Simon and Schuster, 2000.

5. Bennett, R.F.; Hanks, K.; Pulsipher, G.L. *Gaining Control*. Salt Lake City, Utah: Franklin International Institute, Inc., 1987.

6. Muehlhauser, L. *Three Types of Worldview, with Defenders for Each*. Retrieved from <http://commonsenseatheism.com>.

7. Sire, J.W. *The Universe Next Door: A Basic Worldview Catalog*, Fourth Edition. Grove, IL: InterVarsity Press, 1973.

8. Odle, T.G. *A New Generation of Leaders*. Unique Opportunities. The Physician's Resource. January/February 2006. pgs. 14-21.

9. Shapely, D. *Kids Spend Nearly 55 Hours a Week Watching TV, Texting, Playing Video Games...New studies show just how much time children spend consuming media...Here's how to get your kid outside to play*. Retrieved from <http://www.thedailygreen.com/environmental-news/latest/kids-television-47102701>.

10. Barna, *G. Barna Survey Examines Changes in Worldview Among Christians Over the Past 13 years*. Retrieved from http://www.barna.org/barna-update/21-transformation/252-barna-survey-examines-changes-in-worldview-among-christians-over-the-past-14-years#.U7SQwld.

11. Frank, R. *Don't Envy the Superrich They are Miserable*. Retrieved from http://blogs.wsj.com/wealth/2011/03/09/dont-envy-the-super-rich-they-are-miserable/.

12. Mother Teresa quotes. Retrieved from https://www.goodreads.com/author/quotes/838305.Mother Teresa

13. Orwell, G. *1984*. New York: Signet Classics, 1981. pgs 206-207.

14. Harvard Health Publications. *Why behavior change is hard—and why you should keep trying*. Retrieved from <https://www.health.harvard.edu/newsletters/Harvard_Womens_Health_Watch/2012;March/why-behavior-change-is-hard-and-why-you-should-keep-trying>.

15. Abbott, E.A. *Flatland: A Romance of Many Dimensions*. Toronto, Canada: Dover Publications, Inc., 1952.

16. Lee, D. *Plato, The Republic*. New York: Penguin Classics, 1987. pgs. 316-326.

chapter 2

1. Sweats, J. *Evaluation of Diagnostic Systems: Methods from Signal Detection Theory*. New York: Academic Press, Inc., 1982.

2. Sox, H.C. Jr.; Blatt, M.A.; Higgins, M.C.; Marton, K.I. *Medical Decision Making*. Stoneham, MA: Butterworth Publishers, 1988.

3. Dawson-Saunders, B.; Trapp, R.G. *Basic and Clinical Biostatistics*. Norwalk, CT: Appleton & Lange, 1990.

4. Spring, B. *Health Decision making: Lynchpin of Evidence-Based Practice*. Medical Decision Making 2008; 28: 866-874.

5. Taleb, N.N. *The Black Swan: The Impact of the Highly Improbable*. New York: Random House Trade Paperbacks, 2010.

6. Tonstad, S.K. *God of Sense and Traditions of Non-Sense*. Eugene, Oregon: WIPF and Stock, 2016. pgs. 27-28.

7. Dawkins, R. *The Selfish Gene*. New York: Oxford University Press, 2006. p. 20.

8. Rosenberg, A. *The Atheist's Guide to Reality: Enjoying Life without Illusions*. Norton. Kindle edition: Norton and Company, 2011. p. 6.

9. Attributed to Russell in Ted Peters' *Cosmos as Creation: Theology and Science in Consonance* [1989], p. 14, with a note that it was "told [to] a BBC audience [earlier this century]".

10. Loftus, J.W. *The Christian Delusion: Why Faith Fails*. Kindle edition: Prometheus Books, 2012. p. 89.

11. Grant, A. *Give and Take*. New York: Viking Press. 2013.

12. Drucker, P.F. *Management: Tasks, Responsibilities, Practices*. New York: Harper Collins Publishers, 1973. pgs. 38-41.

chapter 3

1. Pellegrino, C. *The Last Train From Hiroshima*. New York: Henry Holt and Company, 2010. pgs. 155-156.

2. Dawson-Saunders, B.; Trapp, R.G. *Basic and Clinical Biostatistics*. Norwalk, CN: Appleton & Lange, 1990.

3. More information about sensitivity and specificity can be obtained by going to the Internet and looking up "Detection theory" and "Signal detection theory." You will note that Dr. Sweats was an important leader in applying the theory to psychological testing and medical decision making.

4. Barker, D. *Believers are no better. Are Christians more moral or successful than non-Christians?* Retrieved from <http://freethoughtpedia.com/wiki/Believers are no better>.

5. Viereck, G.S. *What Life Means to Einstein*. Saturday Evening Post, Oct 26, 1929. p. 117.

6. Mark 10:45. New International Version. 1987.

chapter 4

1. Cheever, J. *The Enormous Radio*. The New Yorker May 17, 1947.

2. Rolheiser, R. *The Restless Heart: Finding Our Spiritual Home in Times of Loneliness*. New York: Doubleday, 2004.

3. Putnam, R.D. *Bowling Alone: The Collapse and Revival of American Community*. New York: Simon and Schuster, 1999. p. 115.

4. Morley, C. Joyce Carol Vincent: *How could this young woman lie dead and undiscovered for almost three years?* Retrieved from https://www.theguardian.com/film/2011/oct/09/joyce-vincent-death-mystery-documentary

5. Thomas, S. *The Legion Lonely*. Retrieved from hazlitt.net/longreads/legion lonely

6. Hawkley, L.C. *Loneliness, Psychosocial States, Behavior, and Cardiovascular Physiology: A 12-hour Field Study*. Ann Arbor, Michigan: University Microfilms International, 2001.

7. Cacioppo, J.T.; Patrick, W. *Loneliness: Human Nature and the Need for Social Connection*. New York: W.W. Norton & Company, 2008.
8. Hafner, K. *Researchers Confront an Epidemic of Loneliness*. New York Times. Sept 5, 2016. p. D1.

9. Peck, M.S. *The Different Drum: Community Making and Peace*. New York: Simon and Schuster, 1987. pgs. 186-200.

10. Little, K. *Cocaine Harms Brain's Pleasure Center*. American Journal of Psychiatry 2003; 160: 1-9.

11. Elmore, T. *How to Build Snowmen from a Snowflake Generation*. https://growingleaders.com/blog/how-to-build-snowmen-from-a-snowflake-generation/

12. Philippians 2: 3, 4. New International Version. 1987.

13. Carlin, J. *Playing the Enemy: Nelson Mandela and the Game That Made a Nation*. New York: Penguin Press, 2008.

14. Pearce, C.L.; Maciariello, J.A.; Yamawaki, H. *The Drucker Difference: What the World's Greatest Management Thinker Means to Today's Business Leaders*. New York: McGraw-Hill Companies, 2010. p. 212.

15. Collins, J. *Good to Great: Why Some Companies Make the Leap…and Others Don't*. New York: Harper Collins, 1958. pgs. 17-38.

16. Fernández-Aráoz, C. *21st Century Talent Spotting*. Harvard Business Review 2014; 92: 2-11.

17. Preston, D. *Skiing with the Dalai Lama*. The Week 2014; 14(666).

chapter 5

1. Tversky, A.; Kahneman, D. *Judgment under uncertainty: Heuristics and Biases*. Science 1974; 185: 1124-1131.

2. Watters, E. *Why Do People Behave Nicely?* Discover. 2005; 26 (12): 38-41.

3. Chapman, G.B.; Elstein A.S. *Cognitive Processes and Biases in Medical Decision Making*. In G.B. Chapman and F.A. Sonnenberg (eds.), *Decision Making in Health Care: Theory, Psychology and Applications*. Cambridge, UK: University of Cambridge. pgs. 183-201.

4. Zeelenberg, M.B.; van der Plight, J.; deVries, N.K. *Consequences of regret aversion: Effects of expected feedback on risky decision making*. Organizational Behavior and Human Decision Processes 1996; 65: 148-158.

5. Kauffman, W. (Edited and translated Nietzsche's *The Gay Science*) The Portable Nietzsche. New York: Viking Books, 1963. p. 95.

6. Berens, L.V.; Nardi, D. *The 16 Sixteen Personality Types: Descriptions for Self-Discovery*. Huntington Beach, CA: Tellos Publications, 1999.

7. McCrae, R.R.; Costa, P.T. *Personality Trait Structure as a Human University*. American Psychologist 1997; 52: 509-516.

8. LaHaye, T. *Your Temperament: Discover its Potential*. Wheaton, Il.: Tyndale House Publishers, Inc., 1984.

9. Gray, J. *Men Are from Mars, Women Are from Venus*. New York: Harper Collins, 1942.

10. Cahill, L. *His Brain, Her Brain*. Scientific American 2005; 242 (5): 40-47.

11. Taylor, K. *She Can Play That Game, Too*. The New York Times. Sunday Styles July 14, 2013. pgs. 1, 2, 6-8.

12. Hammond, J.S.; Keeney, R.L.; Raiffa, H. *Smart Choices: A Practical Guide to Making Better Decisions*. Boston: Harvard Business School Press, 1999; (2000). pgs. 189-216.

13. Redelmeier, D.A.; Shafir, E. *Medical decision making in situations that offer multiple alternatives*. Journal of the American Medical Association 1995; 273(4): 302-305.

14. Iyengar, S.S.; Lepper, M.R. *When Choice is Demotivating: Can One Desire Too Much of a Good Thing?* Journal of Personality and Social Psychology 2000; 79: 995-1006.

15. 1 Corinthians 13:1-10. New International Version. 1987.

16. Wallace, D.F. Kenyon College Graduation Address. Retrieved from Ttps://web.ics.purdue edu/drkelly/DFWKenyonAddress2005.pdf

Chapter 6

1. Nagorski, A. *The Nazi Hunters*. Kindle Edition: Simon & Schuster, 2016. pgs. 629-630.

2. Gino, G. *The Unexpected Influence of Stories Told at Work*. Retrieved from https//hbr.org/2015/09/the-unexpected-influence-of-stories-told-at-work

3. Quartz, S.R.; Sejnowski, T.J. *Liars, Lovers, and Heroes: What the New Brain Science Reveals About How We Become Who We Are*. New York: Harper Collins Publishers, Inc., 2002.

4. Doidge, N. *The Brain That Changes Itself: Stories of Personal Triumph from the Frontiers of Brain Science*. New York: Viking Press, 2007.

5. Merzenich, M. *Soft-Wired: How the New Science of Brain Plasticity Can Change Your Life*. San Francisco, CA: Parnassus Publishing LLC, 2013.

6. Antoinette, N. Retrieved from https://www.nicoleantoinette,com

7. Haidt, J. *The Righteous Mind: Why Good People Are Divided by Politics and Religion*. New York: Random House, Inc., 2012.

8. Harvard Health Publications. *Why behavior change is hard—and why you should keep trying*. Retrieved from <https://www.health.harvard.edu/ newsletters/Harvard_Womens_Health_Watch/2012;March/why-behavior-change-is-hard-and-why-you-should-keep-trying>.

9. Maxwell, G. *Servants or Friends?: Another Look at God*. Redlands, CA: Pine Knoll Publications, 1992.

10. Rizzolatti, G.; Fogassi, L.; Gallese, V. *Mirrors in the Mind. A special class of brain cells reflects the outside world, revealing a new avenue for human understanding, connecting and learning*. Scientific American 2006; 245 (11): 54-69.

11. Dobbs, D.A. *Revealing Reflection. Mirror neurons are providing stunning insights into everything from how we learn to walk to how we empathize with others*. Scientific American Mind 2006; 17 (2): 22-27.

12. Berndt, T.J.; Murphy, L.M. *Influences of Friends and Friendships: Myths, Truths, and Research Recommendations*. Advances in Child Development and Behavior 2002; 30: 275-311.

13. Corwin, N. *Good Can Be as Communicable as Evil*. Retrieved from <http://www.npr.org/templates/story/story.php?storyId=4607744>.

14. Lawrence, J. *Who You Spend Time With Can Tell Big Story*. Press Enterprise.

15. Christakes, N.A.; Fowler, J.H. *Connected: The Surprising Power of Our Social Network*. New York: Little Brown and Company, 2009.

16. Williams, A. *Friends of a Certain Age*. The New York Times. July 15, 2012. pgs. 1, 7.

17. Holmans, J. *The Rise of Dog Identity Politics*. New York Magazine. January 24, 2010. pgs. 8, 16.

18. Boskovic, D. *Paradigm of the Participatory Universe*. Presented at the 38th International Faith and Learning Seminar, Loma Linda, CA. July 2008, 1-21.

19. Kaminer, A. *David Rakoff*. The New York Times Magazine. December 28, 2012. p. 40.

20. Bondi, R.C. *To Love As God Loves*. Minneapolis, MN: Augsburg Fortress Publishers, 1987.

21. Peterson, C.; Seligman, M.E.P. *Character Strengths and Virtues*, New York: Oxford Press, 2004.

22. Seligman, M.E. *Learned Optimism: How to Change Your Mind and Your Life*. New York: Vintage Books, 1990.

23. Kaplan, J. *Saying Thanks: The Importance of Gratitude. Two little words can change your life. Research shows that gratitude is crucial for health and happiness-here's how to make it part of your life*. Retrieved from <http://www.goodhousekeeping.com/health/wellness/saying-thanks>.

24. Marchant, J. Immunology. *The Pursuit of Happiness*. Nature November 27, 2013.

25. Makos, A. Devotion: *An Epic Story of Heroism, Friendship, and Sacrifice*. Kindle Edition: Random House Publishing Group, 2015.

26. Lewis, M. *Coach: Lessons on the Game of Life*. New York: W.W. Norton and Company, 2005.

27. Lewis M. *Coach: Lessons on the Game of Life*. New York: W.W. Norton and Company, 2005. p 77.

28. Lewis, M. *Coach: Lessons on the Game of Life*. New York: W.W. Norton and Company, 2005. p 82.

29. Lewis, M. Coach: *Lessons on the Game of Life.* New York: W.W. Norton and Company, 2005. pgs. 61, 62.

30. Twerski, A.J. *Do Unto Others. How Good Deeds Can Change Your Life.* Kansas City: Andrews McMeel Publishing, 1997.

index

Page numbers followed by f or t indicate figure or tables.